Reprinted 1983 from the 1850 edition.
Cover design © 1980 Time-Life Books Inc.
Library of Congress CIP data following page 247.

SAN FRANCISCO IN NOVEMBER 1849.

NEW YORK. GEO: P. PUTNAM.

BAYARD TAYLOR.

LITH. OF SARONY & MAJOR. N.Y.

ELDORADO,

ADVENTURES IN THE PATH OF EMPIRE:

COMPRISING

A VOYAGE TO CALIFORNIA, VIA PANAMA; LIFE IN SAN FRANCISCO
AND MONTEREY; PICTURES OF THE GOLD REGION, AND
EXPERIENCES OF MEXICAN TRAVEL:

BY

BAYARD TAYLOR,

AUTHOR OF "VIEWS A-FOOT," "RHYMES OF TRAVEL," ETC.

WITH ILLUSTRATIONS BY THE AUTHOR.

VOL. II.

GEORGE P. PUTNAM, 155 BROADWAY.
LONDON: RICHARD BENTLEY.

1850.

LIST OF ILLUSTRATIONS.

C. W. BENEDICT,
Stereotyper and Printer,
201 William st.

CONTENTS OF VOL. II.

CHAPTER I.

A

CHAPTER I.

On my arrival at the Lower Bar, I found Mr. Raney, of Stockton, who had made the journey with the greatest difficulty, the roads being almost impassable. The rainy season had now fairly set in, and as it came a month earlier than usual, the miners, in most cases, were without their winter supplies. Provisions of all kinds had greatly advanced in price, and the cost of freight from Stockton ran up at once to 75 cts. per lb. Flour was sold on the river at $1 per lb. and other articles were in the same proportion. Much anxiety was felt lest the rains should not abate, in which case there would have been a great deal of suffering on all the rivers.

The clouds gradually lowered and settled down on the topmost pines. Towards evening a chill rain came on, and the many gullies on the hill-sides were filled with brown torrents that brawled noisily on their way to the swollen Mokelumne. The big drops splashed dismally on our tent, as we sat within, but a double cover kept us completely dry and the ditch dug inside the pins turned off the streams that poured down its sides. During the night, however, the wind blew violently down the ravines, and the skirts of our blankets nearest the side of the tent were thoroughly soaked. My boots stood under a leaky part of the canvas, and as I hastened to put them on next morning, without examination, I thrust my foot into about three inches of water

The Election Day dawned wet and cheerlessly. From the folds of our canvas door, we looked out on the soaked and trickling hills and the sodden, dripping tents. Few people were stirring about the place, and they wore such a forlorn look that all idea of getting up a special enthusiasm was at once abandoned. There was no motion made in the matter until towards noon, as the most of the miners lay dozing in their tents. The Alcalde acted as Judge, which was the first step; next there were two Inspectors to be appointed. I was requested to act as one, but, although I had been long enough in the country to have held the office, I declined to accept until after application had been made to some of the inhabitants. The acquiescence of two of the resident traders relieved me of the responsibility. The election was held in the largest tent in the place, the Inspectors being seated behind the counter, in close proximity to the glasses and bottles, the calls for which were quite as frequent as the votes. I occupied a seat next the Alcalde, on a rough couch covered with an India-rubber blanket, where I passed the day in looking on the election and studying the singular characters present.

As there were two or three candidates for State offices in the place, the drumming up of voters gave one a refreshing reminiscence of home. The choosing of candidates from lists, nearly all of whom were entirely unknown, was very amusing. Names, in many instances, were made to stand for principles; accordingly, a Mr. Fair got many votes. One of the candidates, who had been on the river a few days previous, wearing a high-crowned silk hat,

with narrow brim, lost about twenty votes on that account. Some
went no further than to vote for those they actually knew. One
who took the opposite extreme, justified himself in this wise :—
" When I left home," said he, " I was determined to *go it blind*.
I went it blind in coming to California, and I'm not going to stop
now. I voted for the Constitution, and I've never seen the Constitution. I voted for all the candidates, and I don't know a
damned one of them. I'm going it blind all through, I am." The
Californians and resident Mexicans who were entitled to vote, were
in high spirits, on exercising the privilege for the first time in
their lives. It made no difference what the ticket was ; the fact
of their having voted very much increased their self-importance,
for the day at least.

The votes polled amounted to one hundred and five, all of which
were " For the Constitution." The number of miners on the
Bar, who were entitled to vote, was probably double this number,
but those who were at work up among the gulches remained in
their tents, on account of the rain. A company on the other side
of the river was completely cut off from the polls by the rise of
the flood, which made it impossible for them to cross. The Inspectors were puzzled at first how far to extend the privilege of
suffrage to the Mexicans. There was no copy of the Treaty of
Queretaro to be had, and the exact wording of the clause referring
to this subject was not remembered. It was at last decided, however, that those who had been residing in the country since the
conquest, and intended to remain permanently, might be admitted
to vote ; and the question was therefore put to each one in turn.
The most of them answered readily in the affirmative, and seemed
delighted to be considered as citizens. " *Como no* ?" said a fat,
good-humored fellow, with a ruddy olive face, as he gave his

sarape a new twirl over his shoulder : " *Como no? soy Americano ahora.*" (Why not? I am now an American.) The candidates, whose interest it was to search out all delinquents, finally exhausted the roll, and the polls were closed. The returns were made out in due form, signed and dispatched by a messenger to the Double Spring, to await the carrier from the Upper Bar, who was to convey them to Stockton.

During the few days I spent on the Mokelumne, I had an opportunity of becoming acquainted with many curious characteristics and incidents of mining life. It would have been an interesting study for a philosopher, to note the different effects which sudden enrichment produced upon different persons, especially those whose lives had previously been passed in the midst of poverty and privation. The most profound scholar in human nature might here have learned something which all his previous wisdom and experience could never teach. It was not precisely the development of new qualities in the man, but the exhibition of changes and contrasts of character, unexpected and almost unaccountable. The world-old moral of gold was completely falsified. Those who were unused to labor, whose daily ounce or two seemed a poor recompense for weary muscles and flagging spirits, might carefully hoard their gains ; but they whose hardy fibre grappled with the tough earth as naturally as if it knew no fitter play, and made the coarse gravel and rocky strata yield up their precious grains, were as profuse as princes and as open-hearted as philanthropists. Weather-beaten tars, wiry, delving Irishmen, and stalwart foresters from the wilds of Missouri, became a race of sybarites and epicureans. Secure in possessing the " Open Sesamé" to the exhaustless treasury under their feet, they gave free rein to every whim or impulse which could possibly be gratified.

It was no unusual thing to see a company of these men, who had never before had a thought of luxury beyond a good beef-steak and a glass of whiskey, drinking their champagne at ten dollars a bottle, and eating their tongue and sardines, or warming in the smoky camp-kettle their tin canisters of turtle-soup and lobster-salad. It was frequently remarked that the Oregonians, though accustomed all their lives to the most simple, solid and temperate fare, went beyond every other class of miners in their fondness for champagne and all kinds of cordials and choice liquors. These were the only luxuries they indulged in, for they were, to a man, cautious and economical in the use of gold.

One of the most amusing cases I saw was that of a company of Englishmen, from New South Wales, who had been on the Moke-lumne about a week at the time of my visit. They had only landed in California two weeks previous, and this was their first experience of gold-digging. One of them, a tall, strong-limbed fellow, who had served seven years as a private of cavalry, was unceasing in his exclamations of wonder and delight. He repeated his story from morning till night, and in the fullness of his heart communicated it to every new face he saw. "By me soul, but this is a great country!" he would exclaim; " here a man can dig up as much goold in a day as he ever saw in all his life. Hav'n't I got already more than I know what to do with, an' I've only been here a week. An' to think 'at I come here with never a single bloody farthing in my pocket! An' the Frenchman, down the hill there, him 'at sells wittles, he wouldn't trust me for a piece of bread, the devil take him! 'If ye 've no money, go an' dig some ;' says he ; ' people dig here o' Sundays all the same.' ' Ill dig o' Sundays for no man, ye bloody villain ;' says I, ' I'll starve first.' An' I did'nt, an' I had a hungry belly, too. But o'

Monday I dug nineteen dollars, an' o' Tuesday twenty-three, an' o' Friday two hundred an' eighty-two dollars in one lump as big as yer fist; an' all for not workin' o' Sundays. Was there ever sich a country in the world!" And, as if to convince himself that he actually possessed all this gold, he bought champagne, ale and brandy by the dozen bottles, and insisted on supplying every body in the settlement.

There was one character on the river, whom I had met on my first visit in August and still found there on my return. He possessed sufficient individuality of appearance and habits to have made him a hero of fiction; Cooper would have delighted to have stumbled upon him. His real name I never learned, but he was known to all the miners by the cognomen of "Buckshot"—an appellation which seemed to suit his hard, squab figure very well. He might have been forty years of age or perhaps fifty; his face was but slightly wrinkled, and he wore a heavy black beard which grew nearly to his eyes and entirely concealed his mouth. When he removed his worn and dusty felt hat, which was but seldom, his large, square forehead, bald crown and serious gray eyes gave him an appearance of reflective intellect;—a promise hardly verified by his conversation. He was of a stout and sturdy frame, and always wore clothes of a coarse texture, with a flannel shirt and belt containing a knife. I guessed from a slight peculiarity of his accent that he was a German by birth, though I believe he was not considered so by the miners.

The habits of "Buckshot" were still more eccentric than his appearance. He lived entirely alone, in a small tent, and seemed rather to shun than court the society of others. His tastes were exceedingly luxurious; he always had the best of everything in the market, regardless of its cost. The finest hams, at a dollar

and a half the pound ; preserved oysters, corn and peas, at six
dollars a canister ; onions and potatoes, whenever such articles
made their appearance ; Chinese sweetmeats and dried fruits, were
all on his table, and his dinner was regularly moistened by a bottle
of champagne. He did his own cooking, an operation which cost
little trouble, on account of the scarcity of fresh provisions. When
particularly lucky in digging, he would take his ease for a day or
two, until the dust was exhausted, when he would again shoulder
his pick and crowbar and commence burrowing in some lonely
corner of the rich gulch. He had been in the country since the
first discovery of the placers, and was reported to have dug, in all,
between thirty and forty thousand dollars,—all of which he had
spent for his subsistence. I heard him once say that he never
dug less than an ounce in one day, and sometimes as much as two
pounds. The rough life of the mountains seemed entirely conge-
nial to his tastes, and he could not have been induced to change
it for any other, though less laborious and equally epicurean.

Among the number of miners scattered through the different gulches, I met daily with men of education and intelligence, from all parts of the United States. It was never
safe to presume on a person's character, from his dress or
appearance. A rough, dirty, sunburnt fellow, with unshorn
beard, quarrying away for life at the bottom of some rocky
hole, might be a graduate of one of the first colleges in the
country, and a man of genuine refinement and taste. I found
plenty of men who were not outwardly distinguishable from th
inveterate trapper or mountaineer, but who, a year before, ha
been patientless physicians, briefless lawyers and half-starved
editors. It was this infusion of intelligence which gave the gold-
hunting communities, notwithstanding their barbaric exterior and

mode of life, an order and individual security which at first sight seemed little less than marvellous.

Since my first visit, the use of quicksilver had been introduced on the river, and the success which attended its application to gold-washing will bring it henceforth into general use. An improved rocker, having three or four lateral gutters in its bottom, which were filled with quicksilver, took up the gold so perfectly, that not the slightest trace of it could be discovered in the refuse earth. The black sand, which was formerly rejected, was washed in a bowl containing a little quicksilver in the bottom, and the amalgam formed by the gold yielded four dollars to every pound of sand. Mr. James, who had washed out a great deal of this sand, evaporated the quicksilver in a retort, and produced a cake of fine gold worth nearly five hundred dollars. The machines sold at one thousand dollars apiece, the owners having wisely taken the precaution to have them patented.

There is no doubt that, by means of quicksilver, much of the soil which has heretofore been passed by as worthless, will give a rich return. The day before my departure, Dr. Gillette washed out several panfuls of earth from the very top of the hills, and found it to contain abundance of fine grains of gold. A heap of refuse earth, left by the common rocker after ten thousand dollars had been washed, yielded still another thousand to the new machine. Quicksilver was enormously high, four dollars a pound having been paid in Stockton. When the mines of Santa Clara shall be in operation, the price will be so much reduced that its use will become universal and the annual golden harvest be thereby greatly increased. It will be many years before all the placers or gold deposits are touched, no matter how large the emigration to California may be. The region in which all the mining operations are now carried on, extending from the base of the proper Sierra Nevada to the plains of Sacramento and San Joaquin, is upwards of five hundred miles in length by fifty in breadth. Towards the head of the Sacramento River gold is also found in the granite formation, and there is every reason to believe that it exists in the valleys and cañons of the great snowy ridge.

I was strongly tempted to take hold of the pick and pan, and try my luck in the gulches for a week or two. I had fully intended, on reaching California, to have personally tested the pleasure of gold-digging, as much for the sake of a thorough experience of life among the placers as from a sly hope of striking on a pocket full of big lumps. The unexpected coming-on of the rainy season, made my time of too much account, besides adding greatly to the hardships of the business. Two or three days' practice is requisite to handle the implements properly, and I had no notion of learning the manipulations without fingering the gold. Once, indeed, I took a butcher-knife, went into one of the forsaken holes in the big gulch, lay on my back as I had seen the other miners do, and endeavored to pick out some yellow grains from the crevices of the crumbling rock. My search was vain, however, and I was indebted to the kindness of some friends for the only specimens I brought away from the Diggings.

CHAPTER II.

I LEFT the Mokelumne River the afternoon following Election Day, and retraced my path to Jackson's Creek, which I reached at dark. Being unhorsed, I resumed my old plodding gait, "packing" my blankets and spurs. I was obliged to walk to the Upper Bar, in order to cross the Mokelumne, whose current was now very deep and rapid. A man named Bills, who kept a brush hotel with a canvas roof, had set up an impromptu ferry, made by nailing a few planks upon four empty barrels, lashed together. This clumsy float was put over by means of a rope stretched from bank to bank. The tendency of the barrels to roll in the swift current, made it very insecure for more than two persons. The same morning, four men who were crossing at once, overbore its delicate equilibrium and were tipped into the water, whence they were rescued with some difficulty. A load of freight met with the same luck just before I reached the ferry. The banks were heaped with barrels, trunks, crates of onions and boxes of liquor, waiting to be taken over, and some of the Mexican arrieros were endeavoring to push their pack-mules into the water and force them to swim. I took my place on the unsteady platform with some doubts of a dry skin, but as we were all careful to keep a plumb line, the passage was made in safety.

I toiled up the windings of a deep gulch, whose loneliness, after I had passed the winter huts of the gold-diggers, was made very impressive by the gathering twilight. The gray rocks which walled it in towards the summit looked dim and spectral under the eaves of the pines, and a stream of turbid water splashed with a melancholy sound into the chasm below. The transparent glimmer of the lighted tents on Jackson's Creek had a cheery look as seen at the bottom of the gulch on the other side of the mountain. I stopped at Cosgrove's tent, where several travelers who had arrived before me were awaiting supper. We sat about the fire and talked of gold-digging, the election and the prospect of supplies for the winter. When Mrs. Cosgrove had finished frying her beef and boiling her coffee, we rolled to the table all the casks, boxes and logs we could find, and sat down to our meal under the open stars. A Chinook Indian from Oregon acted as waiter—an attendance which we would rather have dispensed with. I was offered a raw-hide in one corner of a small storage-tent, and spread my blanket upon it ; the dampness of the earth, however, striking through both hide and blankets, gave me several chills and rheumatic pains of the joints, before morning. The little community established on the knoll numbered about sixty persons. They were all settled there for the winter, though the gold dug did not average more than half an ounce to each man, daily.

Next morning, I crossed the hills to Sutter's Creek, where I found the settlement increased by several new arrivals. From this place my path branched off to the north, crossing several mountain ridges to Amador's Creek, which, like the streams I had already passed, was lined with tents and winter cabins. I questioned several miners about their profits, but could get no satisfactory answer. Singularly enough, it is almost impossible to learn

from the miners themselves, unless one happens to be a near acquaintance, the amount of their gains. If unlucky, they dislike
to confess it; if the contrary, they have good reason for keeping it
secret. When most complaining, they may be most successful.
I heard of one, who, after digging fruitlessly for a week, came
suddenly on a pocket, containing about three hundred dollars.
Seeing a friend approaching, he hastily filled it up with stones, and
began grubbing in the top soil. " Well, what luck ?" inquired
his friend. " Not a damned cent," was the answer, given with a
mock despondency, while the pale face and stammering voice betrayed the cheat at once. Nobody believes you are not a gold-
hunter. He must be a fool, they think, who would go to the
mountains for any other purpose. The questions invariably asked
me were : " Where have you been digging ?" and " Where do
you winter ?" If I spoke of going home soon, the expression
was : " Well, I s'pose you've got your pile ;" or, " You've been
lucky in your prospecting, to get off so soon."

Leaving Amador's Creek, a walk of seven miles took me to
Dry Creek, where I found a population of from two to three hundred, established for the winter. The village was laid out with
some regularity, and had taverns, stores, butchers' shops and
monte tables. The digging was going on briskly, and averaged
a good return. The best I could hear of, was $114 in two
days, contrasted with which were the stories of several who had
got nothing but the fever and ague for their pains. The amount
of sickness on these small rivers during the season had been very
great, and but a small part of it, in my opinion, was to be ascribed
to excesses of any kind. All new countries, it is well known,
breed fever and ague, and this was especially the case in the gold
region, where, before the rains came on, the miner was exposed

to intense heat during the day and was frequently cold under double blankets at night. The water of many of the rivers occasions diarrhœa to those who drink it, and scarcely one out of a hundred emigrants escapes an attack of this complaint.

At all these winter settlements, however small, an alcalde is chosen and regulations established, as near as possible in accordance with the existing laws of the country. Although the authority exercised by the alcalde is sometimes nearly absolute, the miners invariably respect and uphold it. Thus, at whatever cost, order and security are preserved ; and when the State organization shall have been completed, the mining communities, for an extent of five hundred miles, will, by a quiet and easy process, pass into regularly constituted towns, and enjoy as good government and protection as any other part of the State. Nothing in California seemed more miraculous to me than this spontaneous evolution of social order from the worst elements of anarchy. It was a lesson worth even more than the gold.

The settlement on Dry Creek is just on the skirts of the rough mountain region—the country of cañons, gulches, cañadas and divides ; terms as familar in the diggings as " per cent" in Wall-street. I had intended to strike directly across the mountains to the American Fork. The people represented this route to be impracticable, and the jagged ridges, ramparted with rock, which towered up in that direction, seemed to verify the story, so I took the trail for Daly's Ranche, twenty-two miles distant. After passing the Willow Springs, a log hut on the edge of a swamp, the road descended to the lower hills, where it was crossed by frequent streams. I passed on the way a group of Indians who were skinning a horse they had killed and were about to roast. They were well armed and had probably shot the horse while it was grazing. I greeted them with a " buenas dias," which they sullenly returned, adding an " ugh ! ugh !" which might have expressed either contempt, admiration, friendship or fear.

In traveling through these low hills, I passed several companies of miners who were engaged in erecting log huts for the winter. The gravelly bottoms in many places showed traces of their prospecting, and the rocker was in operation where there was sufficient water. When I inquired the yield of gold I could get no satisfactory answer, but the faces of the men betrayed no sign of disappointment. While resting under a leafless oak, I was joined by a boy of nineteen who had been digging on the Dry Creek and was now returning to San Francisco, ague-stricken and penniless. We walked on in company for several hours, under a dull gray sky, which momentarily threatened rain. The hot flush of fever was on his face, and he seemed utterly desponding and disinclined to talk. Towards night, when the sky had grown darker, he declared himself unable to go further, but I encouraged him to keep on until we reached a cabin, where the miners kindly received him for the night.

I met on the road many emigrant wagons, bound for the diggings. They traveled in companies of two and three, joining teams whenever their wagons stuck fast in the mire. Some were obliged to unload at the toughest places, and leave part of their stores on the Plain until they could return from their Winter quarters. Their noon camps would be veritable treasures for my friend Darley, the artist, if he could have seen them. The men were all gaunt, long-limbed Rip Van Winkles, with brown faces, matted hair and beards, and garments which seemed to have grown up with them, for you could not believe they had ever been taken off. The women, who were somewhat more tidy, had suffered less from the journey, but there were still many fine subjects for the pencil among them. In the course of the day I passed about thirty teams.

At night, after a toilsome journey, I reached the Cosumne River, two miles below the diggings. I was wet from the swamps I crossed and the pools I had waded, weary in body, and thoroughly convinced of the impossibility of traveling on the Plains during the rainy season. One would think, from the parched and seamed appearance of the soil in summer, that nothing short of an absolute deluge could restore the usual moisture. A single rain, however, fills up the cracks, and a week of wet weather turns the dusty plain into a deep mire, the hollows into pools, and the stony arroyos into roaring streams. The roads then become impassable for wagons, killing to mules, and terribly laborious for pedestrians. In the loose, gravelly soil on the hilltops, a horse at once sinks above his knees, and the only chance of travel is by taking the clayey bottoms. Where, a month before there had been a *jornada* of twenty miles, arid as the desert, my path was now crossed by fifty streams.

Where the trail struck the river I came upon a small tent, pitched by the roadside, and was hailed by the occupants. They were two young men from Boston, who came out in the summer, went to the North-Fork of the American, prospered in their digging, and were going southward to spend the winter. They were good specimens of the sober, hardy, persevering gold-digger —a class who never fail to make their " piles." I willingly accepted their invitation to spend the night, whereupon they threw another log on the camp-fire, mixed some batter for slap-jacks, and put a piece of salt pork in the pan. We did not remain long about the fire, after my supper was finished. Uniting our store of blankets, we made a bed in common for all three, entirely filling the space covered by the little tent. Two or three showers fell during the night, and the dash of rain on the canvas, so near my head, made doubly grateful the warmth and snugness of our covert.

The morning brought another rain, and the roads grew deeper and tougher. At Coates's Ranche, two miles further, I was ferried across the Cosumne in a canoe. The river was falling, and teams could barely pass. The day previous a wagon and team had been washed several hundred yards down the stream, and the owners were still endeavoring to recover the running works which lay in a deep hole. Several emigrant companies were camped on the grassy bottoms along the river, waiting a chance to cross. At the ranche I found breakfast just on the table, and to be had at the usual price of a dollar and a half; the fare consisted of beef broiled in the fire, coarse bread, frijoles and coffee. The landlady was a German emigrant, but had been so long among the American settlers and native rancheros, that her talk was a three-stranded twist of the different languages. She seemed quite unconscious that she was not talking in a single tongue, for all three came to serve her thought with equal readiness.

I stood in the door some time, deliberating what to do. The sky had closed in upon the plain with a cheerless drizzle, which made walking very uncomfortable, and I could find no promise of a favorable change of weather. My intention had been to visit Mormon Island and afterwards Culloma Mill, on the American Fork. The former place was about thirty miles distant, but the trail was faint and difficult to find ; while, should the rain increase, I could not hope to make the journey in one day. The walk to Sacramento presented an equally dispiriting aspect, but after some questioning and deliberation, I thought it possible that General Morse might have left my gray mare at some of the ranches further down the river, and resolved to settle the question before going further. Within the space of two or three miles I visited three, and came at last to a saw-mill, beyond which there was no habitation for ten miles. The family in an adjoining house seemed little disposed to make my acquaintance ; I therefore took shelter from the rain, which was now pouring fast, in a mud cabin, on the floor of which lay two or three indolent vaqueros They were acquainted with every animal on all the ranches, and unhesitatingly declared that my mare was not among them.

When the rain slacked, I walked back to one of the other ranches, where I found several miners who had taken shelter in a new adobe house, which was partially thatched. We gathered together in a room, the floor of which was covered with wet tulé and endeavored to keep ourselves warm. The place was so chill that I went into the house inhabited by the family, and asked permission to dry myself at the fire. The occupants were two women, apparently sisters, of the ages of eighteen and thirty ; the younger would have been handsome, but for an expression of habitual discontent and general contempt of everything. They made no answer to my request, so I took a chair and sat down near the blaze. Two female tongues, however, cannot long keep silent, and presently the elder launched into a violent anathema against all emi*grants*, as she called them. I soon learned that she had been in the country three years ; that she had at first been living on Bear Creek ; that the overland emigrants, the previous year, having come into the country almost destitute, appropriated some of the supplies which had been left at home while the family was absent gold-hunting ; and, finally, that the fear of being in future plundered of their cattle and wheat had driven them to the banks of the Cosumne, where they had hoped for some security. They were deceived, however ; the emi*grants* troubled them worse than ever, and though they charged a dollar and a half a meal and sometimes cleared fifty dollars a day, still their hatred was no*t* abated.

Most especially did the elder express her resentment against the said emigrants, on account of their treatment of the Indians. I felt disposed at first to agree with her wholly in their condemnation, but it appeared that she was influenced by other motives than those of humanity. " Afore these here emi*grants* come," said she ; " the Injuns were as well-behaved and bidable as could be ; I liked 'em more 'n the whites. When we begun to find gold on the Yuber, we could git 'em to work for us day in and day out, fur next to nothin'. We told 'em the gold was stuff to whitewash houses with, and give 'em a hankecher for a tin-cup full ; but after the emi*grants* begun to come along and put all sorts of notions into their heads, there was no gettin' them to do nothin'."

I took advantage of a break in this streak of " chain lightning," to inquire whether Dr. Gwin and Gen. Morse had recently passed that way ; but they did not know them by name. " Well," said I, " the gentlemen who are trying to get elected." " Yes," rejoined the elder, " *them* people *was* here. They stuck their heads in the door one night and asked if they might have supper and lodgin'. I told 'em no, I guessed they couldn't. Jist then Mr. Kewen come along ; he know'd 'em and made 'em acquainted. Gosh ! but I was mad. I *had* to git supper for 'em *then ;* but if 't'd 'a bin *me*, I'd 'a had more spunk than to eat, after I'd bin told I could'n't." It had been difficult for me to keep a serious countenance before, but now I burst into a hearty laugh, which they took as a compliment to their "spunk." One of the household, a man of some education, questioned me as to the object of my emigration to California, which I explained without reserve. This, however, brought on another violent expression of opinion from the same female. "That's jist the way," said she; "*some* people come here, think they've done great things, and go home and publish all sorts of lies; but they don't know no more'n nothin' in God A'mighty's world, as much as *them* people that's bin here three years." After this declaration I thought it best to retreat to the half-finished adobe house, and remain with my companions in misery. Towards evening we borrowed an axe, with which we procured fuel enough for the night, and built a good fire. A Mexican, driven in by the rain, took out his cards and set up a monte bank of ten dollars, at which the others played with shillings and quarters. I tried to read an odd volume of the "Scottish Chiefs," which I found in the house, but the old charm was gone, and I wondered at the childish taste which was so fascinated with its pages.

We slept together on the earthen floor. All night the rain pattered on the *tulé* thatch, but at sunrise it ceased. The sky was still lowering, and the roads were growing worse so rapidly, that instead of starting across the plains for Mormon Island, the nearest point on the American Fork where the miners were at work, I turned about for Sacramento City, thinking it best to return while there was a chance. A little experience of travel over the saturated soil soon convinced me that my tour in the mountains was over. I could easily relinquish my anticipations of a visit to the mining regions of the American Fork, Bear and Yuba Rivers, for life at the different diggings is very much the same, and the character of the gold deposits does not materially vary; but there had ever been a shining point in the background of all my former dreams of California—a shadowy object to be attained, of which I had never lost sight during my wanderings and from which I could not turn away without a pang of regret and disappointment. This was, a journey to the head of the Sacramento Valley, a sight of the stupendous Shaste Peak, which stands like an obelisk of granite capped with gleaming marble, on the borders of Oregon, and perhaps an exploration of the terrific cañons through which the river plunges in a twenty-mile cataract, from the upper shelf of the mountains. The fragments of description which I had gathered from Oregonians, emigrants and " prospecters" who had visited that region, only made my anticipations more glowing and my purpose more fixed. I knew there was grandeur there, though there might not be gold. Three weeks of rough travel, had the dry season extended to its usual length, would have enabled me to make the journey ; but, like most of the splendid plans we build for ourselves, I was obliged to give it up on the eve of fulfilment. A few days of rain completely washed it out of my imagination, and it was long before I could fill the blank.

I was accompanied by one of the "Iowa Rangers," from Dubuque, Iowa. He had been at work at the Dry Diggings on Weaver's Creek. He was just recovering from the scurvy, and could not travel fast, but was an excellent hand at wading. Before reaching the timber of the American Fork, we crossed thirty or forty streams, many of which were knee-deep. Where they were so wide as to render a leap impossible, my plan was to dash through at full speed, and I generally got over with but a partial saturation : the broad, shallow pools obliged us to stop and pull off our boots. It was one form of the water-cure I did not relish. " If this be traveling in the rainy season," thought I, " I'll have none of it."

On the banks of the American Fork we found a sandy soil and made better progress. Following that beautiful stream through the afternoon, we came at dusk to Sutter's Fort, which was surrounded by a moat of deep mud. I picked my way in the dark to Sacramento City, but was several times lost in its tented labyrinths before I reached Capt. Baker's store—under whose hospitable roof I laid down my pack and took up my abode for several days.

CHAPTER III.

SACRAMENTO CITY was one place by day and another by night; and of the two, its night-side was the most peculiar. As the day went down dull and cloudy, a thin fog gathered in the humid atmosphere, through which the canvas houses, lighted from within, shone with a broad, obscure gleam, that confused the eye and made the streets most familiar by daylight look strangely different. They bore no resemblance to the same places, seen at mid-day, under a break of clear sunshine, and pervaded with the stir of business life. The town, regular as it was, became a bewildering labyrinth of half-light and deep darkness, and the perils of traversing it were greatly increased by the mire and frequent pools left by the rain.

To one, venturing out after dark for the first time, these perils were by no means imaginary. Each man wore boots reaching to the knees—or higher, if he could get them—with the pantaloons tucked inside, but there were pit-falls, into which had he fallen, even these would have availed little. In the more frequented streets, where drinking and gambling had full swing, there was a partial light, streaming out through doors and crimson window-curtains, to guide his steps. Sometimes a platform of plank re-

SACRAMENTO CITY, FROM THE SOUTH.

NEW YORK. GEO. P. PUTNAM.

BAYARD TAYLOR

LITH OF SARONY & MAJOR

ceived his feet ; sometimes he skipped from one loose barrel-stave
to another, laid with the convex-side upward ; and sometimes,
deceived by a scanty piece of scantling, he walked off its further
end into a puddle of liquid mud. Now, floundering in the stiff
mire of the mid-street, he plunged down into a gulley and was
" brought up" by a pool of water ; now, venturing near the houses,
a scaffold-pole or stray beam dealt him an unexpected blow. If
he wandered into the outskirts of the town, where the tent-city of
the emigrants was built, his case was still worse. The briery
thickets of the original forest had not been cleared away, and the
stumps, trunks and branches of felled trees were distributed over
the soil with delightful uncertainty. If he escaped these, the lariats of picketed mules spread their toils for his feet, threatening
entanglement and a kick from one of the vicious animals ; tent-
ropes and pins took him across the shins, and the horned heads of
cattle, left where they were slaughtered, lay ready to gore him at
every step. A walk of any distance, environed by such dangers,
especially when the air was damp and chill, and there was a pos-
sibility of rain at any moment, presented no attractions to the
weary denizens of the place.

A great part of them, indeed, took to their blankets soon after
dark. They were generally worn out with the many excitements
of the day, and glad to find a position of repose. Reading was
out of the question to the most of them when candles were $4 per
lb. and scarce at that ; but in any case, the preternatural activity
and employment of mind induced by the business habits of the
place would have made impossible anything like quiet thought.
I saw many persons who had brought the works of favorite authors
with them, for recreation at odd hours, but of all the works thus
brought, I never saw one read. Men preferred—or rather it grew,

involuntarily, into a custom—to lie at ease instead, and turn over
in the brain all their shifts and manœuvres of speculation, to see
whether any chance had been left uutouched. Some, grouped
around a little pocket-stove, beguile an hour or. two over their
cans of steaming punch or other warming concoction, and build
schemes out of the smoke of their rank Guayaquil *puros*—for the
odor of a genuine Havana is unknown. But, by nine o'clock at
farthest, nearly all the working population of Sacramento City are
stretched out on mattrass, plank or cold earth, according to the
state of their fortunes, and dreaming of splendid runs of luck or
listening to the sough of the wind in the trees.

There is, however, a large floating community of overland emigrants, miners and sporting characters, who prolong the wakeful-
ness of the streets far into the night. The door of many a gam-
bling-hell on the levee, and in J and K streets, stands invitingly
open ; the wail of torture from innumerable musical instruments
peals from all quarters through the fog and darkness. Full bands,
each playing different tunes discordantly, are stationed in front of
the principal establishments, and as these happen to be near together, the mingling of the sounds in one horrid, ear-splitting,
brazen chaos, would drive frantic a man of delicate nerve. All
one's old acquaintances in the amateur-music line, seem to have
followed him. The gentleman who played the flute in the next
room to yours, at home, has been hired at an ounce a night to
perform in the drinking-tent across the way ; the very French
horn whose lamentations used to awake you dismally from the first
sweet snooze, now greets you at some corner ; and all the squeak-
ing violins, grumbling violincellos and rowdy trumpets which have
severally plagued you in other times, are congregated here, in
loving proximity. The very strength, loudness and confusion of

the noises, which, heard at a little distance, have the effect of one great scattering performance, marvellously takes the fancy of the rough mountain men.

Some of the establishments have small companies of Ethiopian melodists, who nightly call upon " Susanna !" and entreat to be carried back to Old Virginny. These songs are universally popular, and the crowd of listeners is often so great as to embarrass the player at the monte tables and injure the business of the gamblers. I confess to a strong liking for the Ethiopian airs, and used to spend half an hour every night in listening to them and watching the curious expressions of satisfaction and delight in the faces of the overland emigrants, who always attended in a body. The spirit of the music was always encouraging ; even its most doleful passages had a grotesque touch of cheerfulness—a mingling of sincere pathos and whimsical consolation, which somehow took hold of all moods in which it might be heard, raising them to the same notch of careless good-humor. The Ethiopian melodies well deserve to be called, as they are in fact, the national airs of America. Their quaint, mock-sentimental cadences, so well suited to the broad absurdity of the words—their reckless gaiety and irreverent familiarity with serious subjects—and their spirit of antagonism and perseverance—are true expressions of the more popular sides of the national character. They follow the American race in all its emigrations, colonizations and conquests, as certainly as the Fourth of July and Thanksgiving Day. The penniless and half-despairing emigrant is stimulated to try again by the sound of " It 'll never do to give it up so !" and feels a pang of home-sickness at the burthen of the " Old Virginia Shore."

At the time of which I am writing, Sacramento City boasted the only theatre in California. Its performances, three times a week, were attended by crowds of the miners, and the owners realized a very handsome profit. The canvas building used for this purpose fronted on the levee, within a door or two of the City Hotel; it would have been taken for an ordinary drinking-house, but for the sign: " EAGLE THEATRE," which was nailed to the top of the canvas frame. Passing through the bar-room we arrive at the entrance; the prices of admission are : Box, $3 ; Pit, $2. The spectators are dressed in heavy overcoats and felt hats, with boots reaching to the knees. The box-tier is a single rough gallery at one end, capable of containing about a hundred persons ; the pit will probably hold three hundred more, so that the receipts of a full house amount to $900. The sides and roof of the theatre are canvas, which, when wet, effectually prevents ventilation, and renders the atmosphere hot and stifling. The drop-curtain, which is down at present, exhibits a glaring landscape, with dark-brown trees in the foreground, and lilac-colored mountains against a yellow sky.

The overture commences ; the orchestra is composed of only five members, under the direction of an Italian, and performs with tolerable correctness. The piece for the night is " The Spectre of the Forest," in which the celebrated actress, Mrs. Ray, " of the Royal Theatre, New Zealand," will appear. The bell rings ; the curtain rolls up ; and we look upon a forest scene, in the midst of which appears Hildebrand, the robber, in a sky-blue mantle. The foliage of the forest is of a dark-red color, which makes a great impression on the spectators and prepares them for the bloody scenes that are to follow. The other characters are a brave knight in a purple dress, with his servant in scarlet ; they are about to storm the robber's hold and carry off a captive maiden. Several acts are filled with the usual amount of fighting and terrible speeches ; but the interest of the play is carried to an awful height by the appearance of two spectres, clad in mutilated tent-covers, and holding spermaceti candles in their hands.   At this juncture Mrs. Ray rushes in and throws herself into an attitude in the middle of the stage : why she does it, no one can tell.   This movement, which she repeats several times in the course of the first three acts, has no connection with the tragedy ; it is evidently introduced for the purpose of showing the audience that there is, actually, a female performer.   The miners, to whom the sight of a woman is not a frequent occurrence, are delighted with these passages and applaud vehemently.

In the closing scenes, where Hildebrand entreats the heroine to become his bride, Mrs. Ray shone in all her glory.   " No !" said she, " I'd rather take a basilisk and wrap its cold fangs around me, than be clasped in the hembraces of an 'artless robber."   Then, changing her tone to that of entreaty, she calls upon the knight in purple, whom she declares to be " me 'ope—me only 'ope !"   We will not stay to hear the songs and duetts which follow; the tragedy has been a sufficient infliction.   For her " 'art-rending" personations, Mrs. Ray received $200 a week, and the wages of the other actors were in the same proportion.   A musical gentle-man was paid $96 for singing " The Sea! the Sea!" in a deep bass voice.   The usual sum paid musicians was $16 a night.   A Swiss organ-girl, by playing in the various hells, accumulated $4000 in the course of five or six months.

The southern part of Sacramento City, where the most of the overland emigrants had located themselves, was an interesting place for a night-ramble, when one had courage to undertake threading the thickets among which their tents were pitched.   There, on fallen logs about their camp-fires, might be seen groups that had

journeyed together across the Continent, recalling the hardships
and perils of the travel. The men, with their long beards,
weather-beaten faces and ragged garments, seen in the red, flickering light of the fires, made wild and fantastic pictures. Sometimes four of them might be seen about a stump, intent on re-
viving their ancient knowledge of "poker," and occasionally a
more social group, filling their tin cups from a kettle of tea or
something stronger. Their fires, however, were soon left to
smoulder away; the evenings were too raw and they were too
weary with the day's troubles to keep long vigils.

Often, too, without playing the eavesdropper, one might mingle
unseen with a great many of their companies gathered together
inside the tents. The thin, transparent canvas revealed the shadows of their forms, and was no impediment to the sound of their
voices; besides, as they generally spoke in a bold, hearty tone,
every word could be overheard at twenty yards' distance. The
fragments of conversation which were caught in walking through
this part of the city made a strange but most interesting medley.
There were narratives of old experience on the Plains; notes
about the passage of the mountains compared; reminiscences of
the Salt Lake City and its strange enthusiasts; sufferings at the
sink of Humboldt's River and in the Salt Desert recalled, and
opinions of California in general, given in a general manner.
The conversation, however, was sure to wind up with a talk
about home—a lamentation for its missed comforts and frequently
a regret at having forsaken them. The subject was inexhaustible,
and when once they commenced calling up the scenes and incidents of their life in the Atlantic or Mississippi world, everything
else was forgotten. At such times, and hearing snatches of these
conversations, I too was carried home by an irresistible longing,

and went back to my blankets and dreams of grizzly bear, discouraged and dissatisfied.

Before I left the place, the number of emigrants settled there for the winter amounted to two or three thousand. They were all located on the vacant lots, which had been surveyed by the original owners of the town and were by them sold to others. The emigrants, who supposed that the land belonged of right to the United States, boldly declared their intention of retaining possession of it. Each man voted himself a lot, defying the threats and remonstrances of the rightful owners. The town was greatly agitated for a time by these disputes ; meetings were held by both parties, and the spirit of hostility ran to a high pitch. At the time of my leaving the country, the matter was still unsettled, but the flood which occurred soon after, by sweeping both squatters and speculators off the ground, balanced accounts for awhile and left the field clear for a new start.

In the gambling-hells, under the excitement of liquor and play, a fight was no unusual occurrence. More than once, while walking in the streets at a late hour, I heard the report of a pistol ; once, indeed, I came near witnessing a horrid affray, in which one of the parties was so much injured that he lay for many days blind, and at the point of death. I was within a few steps of the door, and heard the firing in time to retreat. The punishment for these quarrels, when inflicted—which was very rarely done—was not so prompt and terrible as for theft ; but, to give the gambling community their due, their conduct was much more orderly and respectable than it is wont to be in other countries. This, however, was not so much a merit of their own possessing, as the effect of a strong public sentiment in favor of preserving order.

I must not omit to mention the fate of my old gray mare, who

2*

would have served me faithfully, had she been less lazy and better provided with forage. On reaching Sacramento City I found that Gen. Morse had been keeping her for me at a livery stable, at a cost of $5 a day. She looked in much better spirits than when I saw her eating pine-bark on the Mokelumne, and in riding to the town of Sutter, I found that by a little spurring, she could raise a very passable gallop. The rains, however, by putting a stop to travel, had brought down the price of horses, so that after searching some time for a purchaser I could get no offer higher than $50. I consented to let her go; we went into a store and weighed out the price in fine North Fork gold, and the new owner, after trotting her through the streets for about an hour, sold her again for $60. I did not care to trace her fortunes further.

CHAPTER IV.

THE OVERLAND EMIGRATION OF 1849.

SACRAMENTO CITY was the goal of the emigration by the northern routes. From the beginning of August to the last of December scarcely a day passed without the arrival of some man or company of men and families, from the mountains, to pitch their tents for a few days on the bank of the river and rest from their months of hardship. The vicissitudes through which these people had passed, the perils they had encountered and the toils they had endured seem to me without precedent in History. The story of thirty thousand souls accomplishing a journey of more than two thousand miles through a savage and but partially explored wilderness, crossing on their way two mountain chains equal to the Alps in height and asperity, besides broad tracts of burning desert, and plains of nearly equal desolation, where a few patches of stunted shrubs and springs of brackish water were their only stay, has in it so much of heroism, of daring and of sublime endurance, that we may vainly question the records of any age for its equal. Standing as I was, at the closing stage of that grand pilgrimage, the sight of these adventurers as they came in day by day, and the hearing of their stories, each of which had its own peculiar and separate character, had a more fascinating, because more real interest than the tales of the glorious old travelers which so impress us in childhood.

It would be impossible to give, in a general description of the emigration, viewed as one great movement, a complete idea of its many wonderful phases. The experience of any single man, which a few years ago would have made him a hero for life, becomes mere common-place, when it is but one of many thousands ; yet the spectacle of a great continent, through a region of one thousand miles from north to south, being overrun with these adventurous bands, cannot be pictured without the relation of many episodes of individual bravery and suffering. I will not attempt a full account of the emigration, but, as I have already given an outline of the stories of those who came by the Gila route, a similar sketch of what those encountered who took the Northern route —the great overland highway of the Continent—will not be without its interest in this place.

The great starting point for this route was Independence, Mo., where thousands were encamped through the month of April, waiting until the grass should be sufficiently high for their cattle, before they ventured on the broad ocean of the Plains. From the first of May to the first of June, company after company took its departure from the frontier of civilization, till the emigrant trail from Fort Leavenworth, on the Missouri, to Fort Laramie, at the foot of the Rocky Mountains, was one long line of mule-trains and wagons. The rich meadows of the Nebraska, or Platte, were settled for the time, and a single traveler could have journeyed for the space of a thousand miles, as certain of his lodging and regular meals as if he were riding through the old agricultural districts of the Middle States. The wandering tribes of Indians on the Plains —the Pawnees, Sioux and Arapahoes—were alarmed and bewildered by this strange apparition. They believed they were about to be swept away forever from their hunting-grounds and graves.

As the season advanced and the great body of the emigrants got under way, they gradually withdrew from the vicinity of the trail and betook themselves to grounds which the former did not reach. All conflicts with them were thus avoided, and the emigrants passed the Plains with perfect immunity from their thievish and hostile visitations.

Another and more terrible scourge, however, was doomed to fall upon them. The cholera, ascending the Mississippi from New Orleans, reached St. Louis about the time of their departure from Independence, and overtook them before they were fairly embarked on the wilderness. The frequent rains of the early spring, added to the hardship and exposure of their travel, prepared the way for its ravages, and the first three or four hundred miles of the trail were marked by graves. It is estimated that about four thousand persons perished from this cause. Men were seized without warning with the most violent symptoms, and instances occurred in which the sufferer was left to die alone by the road-side, while his panic-stricken companions pushed forward, vainly trusting to get beyond the influence of the epidemic. Rough boards were planted at the graves of those who were buried near the trail, but there are hundreds of others lying unmarked by any memorial, on the bleak surface of the open plain and among the barren depths of the mountains. I have heard men tell how they have gone aside from their company to bury some old and cherished friend—a brother, it may often have been—performing the last rites alone and un-aided, and leaving the remains where none but the wolf will ever seek their resting-place.

By the time the companies reached Fort Laramie the epidemic had expended its violence, and in the pure air of the elevated mountain region they were safe from its further attacks. Now, however, the real hardships of their journey began. Up and down the mountains that hem in the Sweetwater Valley—over the spurs of the Wind River chain—through the Devil's Gate, and past the stupendous mass of Rock Independence—they toiled slowly up to the South Pass, descended to the tributaries of the Colorado and plunged into the rugged defiles of the Timpanozu Mountains. Here the pasturage became scarce and the companies were obliged to take separate trails in order to find sufficient grass for their teams. Many, who, in their anxiety to get forward with speed, had thrown away a great part of the supplies that encumbered them, now began to want, and were frequently reduced, in their necessity, to make use of their mules and horses for food. It was not unusual for a mess, by way of variety to the tough mule-meat, to kill a quantity of rattle-snakes, with which the mountains abounded, and have a dish of them fried, for supper. The distress of many of the emigrants might have been entirely avoided, had they possessed any correct idea, at the outset of the journey, of its length and privations.

It must have been a remarkable scene, which the City of the Great Salt Lake presented during the summer. There, a community of religious enthusiasts, numbering about ten thousand, had established themselves beside an inland sea, in a grand valley shut in by snow-capped mountains, a thousand miles from any other civilized spot, and were dreaming of rebuilding the Temple and creating a New Jerusalem. Without this resting-place in mid-journey, the sufferings of the emigrants must have been much aggravated. The Mormons, however, whose rich grain-lands in the Valley of the Utah River had produced them abundance of supplies, were able to spare sufficient for those whose stock was exhausted. Two or three thousand, who arrived late in the season, remained in the Valley all winter, fearing to undertake the toilsome journey which still remained.

Those who set out for California had the worst yet in store for them. Crossing the alternate sandy wastes and rugged mountain chains of the Great Basin to the Valley of Humboldt's River, they were obliged to trust entirely to their worn and weary animals for reaching the Sierra Nevada before the winter snows. The grass was scarce and now fast drying up in the scorching heat of midsummer. In the endeavor to hasten forward and get the first chance of pasture, many again committed the same mistake of throwing away their supplies. I was told of one man, who, with a refinement of malice and cruelty which it would be impossible to surpass, set fire to the meadows of dry grass, for the sole purpose, it was supposed, of retarding the progress of those who were behind and might else overtake him. A company of the emigrants, on the best horses which were to be obtained, pursued him and shot him from the saddle as he rode—a fate scarcely equal to his deserts.

The progress of the emigrants along the Valley of Humboldt's River is described as having been slow and toilsome in the extreme. The River, which lies entirely within the Great Basin,— whose waters, like those of the uplands of Central Asia, have no connexion with the sea—shrinks away towards the end of summer, and finally loses itself in the sand, at a place called the Sink. Here, the single trail across the Basin divides into three branches, and the emigrants, leaving the scanty meadows about the Sink, have before them an arid desert, varying from fifty to eighty miles in breadth, according to the route which they take. Many companies, on arriving at this place, were obliged to stop and recruit their exhausted animals, though exposed to the danger of being detained there the whole winter, from the fall of snow on the Sierra Nevada. Another, and very large body of them, took the upper route to Lawson's Pass, which leads to the head of the Sacramento Valley ; but the greater part, fortunately, chose the old traveled trails, leading to Bear Creek and the Yuba, by way of Truckee River, and to the head-waters of the Rio Americano by way of Carson's River.

The two latter routes are the shortest and best. After leaving the Sink of Humboldt's River, and crossing a desert of about fifty miles in breadth, the emigrant reaches the streams which are fed from the Sierra Nevada, where he finds good grass and plenty of game. The passes are described as terribly rugged and precipitous, leading directly up the face of the great snowy ridge. As, however, they are not quite eight thousand feet above the sea, and are reached from a plateau of more than four thousand feet, the ascent is comparatively short ; while, on the western side, more than a hundred miles of mountain country must be passed, before reaching the level of the Sacramento Valley. There are frequent passes in the Sierra Nevada which were never crossed before the summer of 1849. Some of the emigrants, diverging from the known trail, sought a road for themselves, and found their way down from the snows to the head waters of the Tuolumne, the Calaveras and Feather River. The eastern slope of the Sierra Nevada is but imperfectly explored. All the emigrants concurred in representing it to me as an abrupt and broken region, the higher peaks of barren granite, the valleys deep and narrow, yet in many places timbered with pine and cedar of immense growth.

After passing the dividing ridge,—the descent from which was rendered almost impossible by precipices and steeps of naked rock —about thirty miles of alternate cañons and divides lay between the emigrants and the nearest diggings. The steepness of the slopes of this range is hardly equalled by any other mountains in the world. The rivers seem to wind their way through the bottoms of chasms, and in many places it is impossible to get down to the water. The word cañon (meaning, in Spanish, a funnel,) has a peculiar adaptation to these cleft channels through which the rivers are poured. In getting down from the summit ridge the emigrants told me they were frequently obliged to take the oxen from the wagon and lower it with ropes ; but for the sheer descents which followed, another plan was adopted. The wheels were all locked, and only one yoke of oxen left in front ; a middling-sized pine was then cut down, and the butt fastened to the axle-tree, the branchy top dragging on the earth. The holding back of the oxen, the sliding of the locked wheels, and the resistance of the tree together formed an opposing power sufficient to admit of a slow descent ; but it was necessary to observe great care lest the pace should be quickened, for the slightest start would have overcome the resistance and given oxen, wagon and tree together a momentum that would have landed them at the bottom in a very different condition.

In August, before his departure for Oregon, Gen. Smith took the responsibility of ordering pack-mules and supplies to be provided at the expense of Government, and gave Major Rucker orders to dispatch relief companies into the Great Basin to succor the emigrants who might be remaining there, for want of provisions to advance further. In this step he was also warmly seconded by Gen. Riley, and the preparations were made with the least possible delay. Public meetings of the citizens of San Francisco were also held, to contribute means of relief. Major Rucker dispatched a party with supplies and fresh animals by way of the

Truckee River route to the Sink of Humboldt's River, while he took the expedition to Pitt River and Lawson's Pass, under his own command. The first party, after furnishing provisions on the road to all whom they found in need, reached the Sink, and started the families who were still encamped there, returning with them by the Carson River route and bringing in the last of the emigration, only a day or two before the heavy snows came on, which entirely blocked up the passes. But for this most timely aid, hundreds of persons must have perished by famine and cold.

Those who took the trail for Lawson's Pass fared even worse. They had been grossly deceived with regard to the route, which, instead of being a nearer passage into California, is actually two hundred miles longer than the other routes, and though there is no ridge of equal height to be crossed, the amount of rough mountain travel is even greater. The trail, after crossing the Sierra by a low gap, (which has lately been mentioned in connection with the Pacific Railroad,) enters the Valley of Pitt River, one of the tributaries of the Upper Sacramento. Following the course of this river for about ninety miles, it reaches a spur of the Sierra Nevada, which runs from the head waters of Feather River to near the Shaste Peak, closing up the level of the lower Sacramento Valley. These mountains are from five to six thousand feet in height and rugged in the extreme, and over them the weary emigrant must pass before the Land of Promise—the rich Valley of the Sacramento—meets his view.

At the time I returned to Sacramento City, Major Rucker had just returned from his expedition. He found a large body of emigrants scattered along Pitt River, many of them entirely destitute of provisions and others without their animals, which the predatory Indians of that region had stolen. Owing to the large number who required his assistance, he was obliged to return to the ranches on Deer Creek and procure further supplies, leaving Mr. Peoples to hurry them on meanwhile. Everything was done to hasten their movement, but a strange and unaccountable apathy seemed to have taken possession of them. The season was late, and a single day added to the time requisite to get them into the Sacramento Valley might prove ruinous to them and their assistants. Whether the weary six months they passed in the wilderness had had the effect of destroying all their active energy and care for their own safety, or whether it was actual ignorance of their true situation and contempt of counsel because it seemed to wear the shape of authority, it is difficult to tell—but the effect was equally dangerous. After having improvidently thrown away, in the first part of the journey, the supplies so needful afterwards, they now held fast to useless goods, and refused to lighten the loads of their tired oxen. But few of them appeared to have a sense of the aid which was rendered them; instead of willingly coöperating with those who had charge of the relief party, they gave much unnecessary trouble and delayed the journey several days.

Of the companies which came by this route several small parties struck into the mountains to the southward of Pitt River, hoping to find an easy road to the diggings on Feather River. Of these, some reached the river, after many days of suffering and danger; others retraced their steps and by making desperate efforts regained the companies on Pitt River, while some, who had not been heard of at the time I left, were either locked up for the winter in the midst of terrible snows, or had already perished from hunger. I met with one or two who had been several days in the mountains without food, and only escaped death by a miracle. A company of six, who set out on the hunt of some Indians who had stolen their cattle, never returned.

It happened to the emigrants as Major Rucker had forewarned them. A letter from Mr. Peoples, which he received during my stay, gave a most striking account of the hardships to which they had subjected themselves. A violent storm came on while they were crossing the mountains to Deer Creek, and the mules, unaccustomed to the severe cold, sank down and died one after another. In spite of their remonstrances, Mr. Peoples obliged them to leave their wagons and hurry forward with the remaining animals. The women, who seemed to have far more energy and endurance than the men, were mounted on mules, and the whole party pushed on through the bleak passes of the mountains in the face of a raging storm. By extraordinary exertions, they were all finally brought into the Sacramento Valley, with the loss of many wagons and animals. On receiving this letter, Major Rucker set out for Lawson's Ranche on Deer Creek, where he saw the emigrants comfortably established for the winter. They had erected log-houses for shelter ; the flour supplied to them from the Government stores and cattle from the large herds on the neighboring ranches, furnished them with the means of subsistence. The return to Sacramento City, in the depth of the rainy season, was an almost impossible undertaking.

The greater part of those who came in by the lower routes, started, after a season of rest, for the mining region, where many of them arrived in time to build themselves log huts for the winter. Some pitched their tents along the river, to wait for the genial spring season ; while not a few took their axes and commenced the business of wood-cutting in the timber on its banks. When shipped to San Francisco, the wood, which they took with the usual freedom of Uncle Sam's nephews, brought $40 a cord ; the steamboats which called for it on their trips up and down, paid $15. By the end of December the last man of the overland companies was safe on the western side of the Sierra Nevada, and the great interior wilderness resumed its ancient silence and solitude until the next spring.

CHAPTER V.

AT the end of a week of rain, during which we had a few deceptive gleams of clear weather, I gave up all hope of getting to the Yuba and Feather Rivers, and took my passage in the steamer Senator, for San Francisco. The time for leaving was before sunrise, and the loud ringing of the first bell awoke me as I lay on my Chinese quilt in Capt. Baker's store. The weather had changed during the night, and when I went out of doors I found a keen, cloudless dawn, with the wind blowing down the river. Had the three weeks of dry season, so confidently predicted by the old settlers, actually commenced? I was not long in deliberating, though the remote chance of an opportunity for making my journey to the Shaste Peak, tempted me sorely; but the end proved that I decided aright, for on the second day after my arrival at San Francisco, the rains set in again worse than ever.

The steamer, which formerly ran between Boston and Eastport, was a strong, spacious and elegant boat. Notwithstanding the fare to San Francisco was $30, she rarely carried less than two hundred passengers. When I went on board, her decks were already filled, and people were hurrying down from all parts of the town, her bell tolling meanwhile with the quick, incessant stroke of a Hudson River boat, one minute before the time of starting. After my recent barbaric life, her long upper saloon, with its sofas and faded carpet, seemed splendid enough for a palace. As we sped down the Sacramento, and the well-known bell and sable herald made their appearance, requesting passengers to step to the Captain's office, I could scarcely believe that I was in California. On the hurricane deck I met with several persons who had been fellow-passengers on the Atlantic and Pacific. Some had been to the head of the Sacramento Valley; some on Feather River; some again on the famous Trinity, where they had got more fever than gold; but all, though not alike successful, seemed energetic and far from being discouraged.

After passing the town of Sutter, the bell rang for breakfast, and having previously procured a ticket for two dollars, I joined the anxious throng who were pressing down the cabin stairs. The long tables were set below in the same style as at home; the fare was abundant and well prepared; even on the Hudson it would have given rise to few grumblings. We steamed rapidly down the river, with Monte Diablo far before us. Owing to the twists and turns of the stream, it was but an uncertain landmark, now appearing on one side and now on the other. The cold snows of the Sierra Nevada were faintly seen in the eastern sky, but between the Sacramento and the mountains, the great plain stretched out in a sweep which to the north and south ran unbroken to the horizon. The banks, stripped now of their summer foliage, would have been dreary and monotonous, but for the tents and log-houses of the settlers and wood-cutters. I noticed in little spots where the thicket had been cleared away, patches of cabbages and other hardy vegetables, which seemed to have a thrifty growth.

We came at last to the entrance of the slough, the navigation of which was a matter of considerable nicety. The current was but a few feet wider than the steamer, and many of the bends occasioned her considerable trouble. Her bow sometimes ran in among the boughs of the trees, where she could not well be backed without her stern going into the opposite bank. Much time and part of the planking of her wheel-houses were lost in getting through these narrow straits. The small craft on their way up the river were obliged to run close under the limbs of the trees and hug the banks tightly until we had passed. At last we came out again in the real Sacramento, avoiding the numerous other sloughs which make off into the tulé marshes, and soon reached the city of Montezuma, a solitary house on a sort of headland projecting into Suisun Bay and fronting its rival three-house city, New-York-of-the-Pacific. The bay was dancing to the fresh northern breeze as we skimmed its waters towards Benicia; Monte Diablo, on the other side, wore a blue mist over his scarred and rocky surface, which looked deceptively near.

The three weeks of rain which had fallen since I passed up the bay, had brought out a vivid green over all the hills. Those along the water were no longer lifeless and barren, but covered with sprouting vegetation. Benicia, as we approached it, appeared like a child's toy town set out on a piece of green velvet. Contrasted with this gay color, the changeless hue of the evergreen oaks appeared sombre almost to blackness; seen in unison with a cloudless sky and the glittering blue of the bay, the effect of the fresh green was indescribably cheerful and inspiring. We touched but a few minutes at Benicia, whose streets presented a quiet appearance, coming from the thronged avenues of Sacramento City. The houses were mostly frame, of neat construction; a church with a small white spire, at the upper end of the town, stood out brightly against the green of the hills behind.

Beyond these hills, at the distance of thirty-five miles, is the pleasant little town of Sonoma, Gen. Vallejo's residence. In summer it is reached from Sacramento City by a trail of forty miles, but when the rains come on, the tulé marshes running up from the bay between the river and the mountains, are flooded, and a circuit of more than a hundred miles must be made to get around them. Two days' journey north of Sonoma is Lake Clear, a beautiful sheet of water, sixty miles in length, embosomed in the midst of grand mountain scenery.

Sunset came on as we approached the strait opening from Pablo Bay into the Bay of San Francisco. The cloudless sky became gradually suffused with a soft rose-tint, which covered its whole surface, painting alike the glassy sheet of the bay, and glowing most vividly on the mountains to the eastward. The color deepened every moment, and the peaks of the Coast Range burned with a rich vermilion light, like that of a live coal. This faded gradually into as glowing a purple, and at last into a blue as intense as that of the sea at noonday. The first effect of the light was most wonderful ; the mountains stretched around the horizon like a belt of varying fire and amethyst between the two roseate deeps of air and water ; the shores were transmuted into solid, the air into fluid gems. Could the pencil faithfully represent this magnificent transfiguration of Nature, it would appear utterly unreal and impossible to eyes which never beheld the reality. It was no transient spectacle, fading away ere one could feel its surpassing glory. It lingered, and lingered, changing almost imperceptibly and with so beautiful a decay, that one lost himself in the enjoyment of each successive charm, without regret for those which

were over. The dark blue of the mountains deepened into their
night-garb of dusky shadow without any interfusion of dead ashy
color, and the heaven overhead was spangled with all its stars long
before the brilliant arch of orange in the west had sunk below the
horizon. I have seen the dazzling sunsets of the Mediterranean
flush the beauty of its shores, and the mellow skies which Claude
used to contemplate from the Pincian Hill; but, lovely as they
are in my memory, they seem cold and pale when I think of the
splendor of such a scene, on the Bay of San Francisco.

The approach to the city was very imposing in the dusk. The
crowd of shipping, two or three miles in length, stretched along
the water in front; the triple crown of the hills behind was clearly
marked against the sky, and from the broad space covered with
sparkling lights, glimmerings of tents and white buildings, and
the sounds of active life, I half believed that some metropolis of a
century's growth lay before me. On landing, notwithstanding I
had only been absent three weeks, I had some difficulty in recognizing localities. The change appeared greater than at any previous arrival, on account of the removal of a great many of the
old buildings and the erection of larger and more substantial edifices in their stead.

After a few days of violent rain, the sky cleared and we had a
week of the most delicious weather I ever experienced. The temperature was at no time lower than 50°, and in the middle of the
day rose to 70°. When the floating gauze of mist had cleared off
the water, the sky was without a cloud for the remainder of the
day, and of a fresh, tender blue, which was in exquisite relief to
the pale green of the hills. To enjoy the delightful temperature
and fine scenery of the Bay, I used frequently to climb a hill just
in the rear of the town, whence the harbor, the strait into Pablo

Bay, the Golden Gate and the horizon of the Pacific could all be seen at one view. On the top of the hill are the graves of several Russians, who came out in the service of the Russian Company, each surmounted with a black cross, bearing an inscription in their language. All this ground, however, has been surveyed, staked into lots and sold, and at the same rate of growth the city will not be long in climbing the hill and disturbing the rest of the Muscovites.

In company with my friends, the Moores, I made many short excursions among the hills, during this charming season. Our most frequent trip was to Fresh Pond, in the neighborhood of the old Presidio. With a gray donkey—an invaluable beast, by the way—harnessed to a light cart, in which we had placed two or three empty barrels, we drove out to the place, a little basin shut in by the hills, and only divided by a narrow bushy ridge from the waters of the Golden Gate. Several tents were pitched on its margin ; the washmen and gardeners had established themselves there and were diligently plying their respective occupations. A little strip of moist bottom adjoining the pond had been cleared of its thickets and was partly ploughed, showing a rich black loam. The washerwomen, of whom there were a few, principally Mexicans and Indians, had established themselves on one side of the pond and the washmen on another. The latter went into the business on a large scale, having their tents for ironing, their large kettles for boiling the clothes and their fluted wash-boards along the edge of the water. It was an amusing sight to see a great, burly, long-bearded fellow, kneeling on the ground, with sleeves rolled up to the elbows, and rubbing a shirt on the board with such violence that the suds flew and the buttons, if there were any, must soon snap off. Their clear-starching and ironing were still more ludicrous ; but, notwithstanding, they succeeded fully as well as the women, and were rapidly growing rich from the profits of their business. Where $8 a dozen is paid for washing clothes, it is very easy to earn double the wages of a Member of Congress.

The sunsets we saw from the hills as we drove slowly back with the barrels filled, were all of the same gorgeous character. The air had a purity and sweetness which made the long hour of twilight enchanting, and we frequently lingered on the road till after dark. We helped our patient donkey up the hill by pushing behind his cart—an aid he seemed fully to appreciate, for he pulled at such times with much more spirit. He had many curious ways about him, the most remarkable of which was his capacity for digestion. Cloth, canvas and shavings seemed as much his natural food as hay or green grass. Whenever he broke loose during the night, which was not seldom, it was generally followed in the morning by a visit from some emigrant, claiming damages for the amount of tent-covering which had been chewed up. Once, indeed, a man who had indulged rather freely in bad brandy, at twenty-five cents a glass, wandered in the dark to the place where the donkey was tethered, lay down at his feet and fell asleep. When he awoke in the morning, sobered by the coolness of his bed and foggy blankets, he found to his utter surprise and horror, that the ravenous beast had not only devoured his cap but cropped nearly all the hair from one side of his head ! As the man's hair happened to be glowing in color and coarse in texture, the mistake of the donkey in taking it to be swamp hay, is not so much to be wondered at.

The valley about the Mission Dolores was charmingly green and beautiful at this time. Several of the former miners, in anticipation of the great influx of emigrants into the country and a consequent market for vegetables, pitched their tents on the best spots along the Mission Creek, and began preparing the ground for gardens. The valley was surveyed and staked into lots almost to the summit of the mountains, and the operation of squatting was performed even by many of the citizens of San Francisco, for the purpose of obtaining titles to the land. Some gentlemen of my acquaintance came into the possession of certain stone quarries, meadow lands and fine sheep-pastures, in this manner; whereupon a friend of mine, and myself, concluded to try the experiment, thinking the experience might, at least, be of some benefit. So, one fine morning we rode out to the Mission, where we found the surveyor on one of the hills, chopping up the chapparal into " hundred vara" lots. He received us cordially, and on looking over his map of the locality, found two adjoining lots of two hundred varas each, which were still unoccupied. They lay on the western side of the Valley, on the slope of the mountains. We hastened away, crossed two yawning arroyos and climbed the steep, where, truly enough, we found the stakes indicating the limits of the survey. I chose a little valley, scooped out between two peaks of the ridge, and watered by a clear stream which trickled down through its centre. My friend took a broader tract, which was not so well watered as mine ; however, on examining the soil, we agreed that it would produce good crops of cabbages and turnips. Accordingly, we marched leisurely over the ground, ascended to its highest part, and took a seat on a boulder of gray rock, which stood exactly upon the line between our two territories. All the beautiful Valley lay beneath us, with the bay beyond, a part of the shipping of San Francisco, and Monte Diablo in the distance—a fine prospect for a squatter !

On our return to the city, we debated whether we should procure materials for a tent and take up an abode on the lofty lots ; but, as it was not at all clear that any land could be granted, or that it would be worth taking even if we should become bona fide settlers, we finally determined to let the matter rest.   We did not repeat our visit, and we learned soon afterwards that violent disputes had arisen between the inhabitants of the Mission and the emigrants who had commenced gardening.   I, who never owned a rood of land in my life, would nevertheless have accepted the proprietorship of one of the bleak pinnacles of the Sierra Navada— or better, the top of the Shaste Peak—could it have been given me, for the mere satisfaction of feeling that there was one spot of the Earth which I might claim as my own, down to its burning centre.

PORTSMOUTH SQUARE, SAN FRANCISCO.

NEW YORK, GEO. P. PUTNAM.

LITH OF SARONY & MAJOR.

CHAPTER VI.

OF all the marvellous phases of the history of the Present, the growth of San Francisco is the one which will most tax the belief of the Future. Its parallel was never known, and shall never be beheld again. I speak only of what I saw with my own eyes. When I landed there, a little more than four months before, I found a scattering town of tents and canvas houses, with a show of frame buildings on one or two streets, and a population of about six thousand. Now, on my last visit, I saw around me an actual metropolis, displaying street after street of well-built edifices, filled with an active and enterprising people and exhibiting every mark of permanent commercial prosperity. Then, the town was limited to the curve of the Bay fronting the anchorage and bottoms of the hills. Now, it stretched to the topmost heights, followed the shore around point after point, and sending back a long arm through a gap in the hills, took hold of the Golden Gate and was building its warehouses on the open strait and almost fronting the blue horizon of the Pacific. Then, the gold-seeking sojourner lodged in muslin rooms and canvas garrets, with a philosophic lack of furniture, and ate his simple though substantial fare from pine boards. Now, lofty hotels, gaudy with verandas and balconies, were met with in all quarters, furnished with home luxury, and aristocratic restaurants presented daily their long bills of fare, rich with the choicest technicalities of the Parisian cuisine. Then, vessels were coming in day after day, to lie deserted and useless at their anchorage. Now scarce a day passed, but some cluster of sails, bound *outward* through the Golden Gate, took their way to all the corners of the Pacific. Like the magic seed of the Indian juggler, which grew, blossomed and bore fruit before the eyes of his spectators, San Francisco seemed to have accomplished in a day the growth of half a century.

When I first landed in California, bewildered and amazed by what seemed an unnatural standard of prices, I formed the opinion that there would be before long a great crash in speculation. Things, it appeared then, had reached the crisis, and it was pronounced impossible that they could remain stationary. This might have been a very natural idea at the time, but the subsequent course of affairs proved it to be incorrect. Lands, rents, goods and subsistence continued steadily to advance in cost, and as the credit system had been meanwhile prudently contracted, the character of the business done was the more real and substantial. Two or three years will pass, in all probability, before there is a positive abatement of the standard of prices. There will be fluctuations in the meantime, occasioning great gains and losses, but the fall in rents and real estate, when it comes, as it inevitably must in the course of two or three years, will not be so crushing as I at first imagined. I doubt whether it will seriously injure the commercial activity of the place. Prices will never fall to the same standard as in the Atlantic States. Fortunes will always be made by the sober, intelligent, industrious, and energetic ; but no one who is either too careless, too spiritless or too ignorant to succeed at home, need trouble himself about emigrating. The same general rule holds good, as well here as elsewhere, and it is all the better for human nature that it is so.

Not only was the heaviest part of the business conducted on cash principles, but all rents, even to lodgings in hotels, were required to be paid in advance. A single bowling-alley, in the basement story of the Ward House—a new hotel on Portsmouth-Square—prepaid $5,000 monthly. The firm of Findley, Johnson & Co. sold their real estate, purchased a year previous, for $20,000, at $300,000 ; $25,000 down, and the rest in monthly instalments of $12,500. This was a fair specimen of the speculations daily made. Those on a lesser scale were frequently of a very amusing character, but the claims on one's astonishment were so constant, that the faculty soon wore out, and the most unheard-of operations were looked upon as matters of course. Among others that came under my observation, was one of a gentleman who purchased a barrel of alum for $6, the price in New York being $9. It happened to be the only alum in the place, and as there was a demand for it shortly afterwards, he sold the barrel for $150. Another purchased all the candle-wick to be found, at an average price of 40 cts. per lb., and sold it in a short time at $2 25 per lb. A friend of mine expended $10,000 in purchasing barley, which in a week brought $20,000. The greatest gains were still made by the gambling tables and the eating-houses. Every device that art could suggest was used to swell the custom of the former. The latter found abundant support in the necessities of a large floating population, in addition to the swarm of permanent residents.

For a month or two previous to this time, money had been very scarce in the market, and from ten to fifteen per cent. monthly, was paid, with the addition of good security. Notwithstanding the quantity of coin brought into the country by emigrants, and the millions of gold dust used as currency, the actual specie basis was very small compared with the immense amount of business transacted. Nevertheless, I heard of nothing like a failure ; the principal firms were prompt in all their dealings, and the chivalry of Commerce—to use a new phrase—was as faithfully observed as it could have been in the old marts of Europe and America. The merchants had a 'Change and News-room, and were beginning to cooperate in their movements and consolidate their credit. A stock company which had built a long wharf at the foot of Sacraento-st. declared a dividend of ten per cent. within six weeks after the wharf was finished. During the muddy season, it was the only convenient place for landing goods, and as the cost of constructing it was enormous, so were likewise the charges for wharfage and storage.

There had been a vast improvement in the means of living since my previous visit to San Francisco. Several large hotels had been opened, which were equal in almost every respect to houses of the second class in the Atlantic cities. The Ward House, the Graham House, imported bodily from Baltimore, and the St. Francis Hotel, completely threw into the shade all former establishments. The rooms were furnished with comfort and even luxury, and the tables lacked few of the essentials of good living, according to a ' home' taste. The sleeping apartments of the St. Francis were the best in California. The cost of board and lodging was $150 per month—which was considered unusually cheap. A room at the Ward House cost $250 monthly, without board. The principal restaurants charged $35 a week for board, and there were lodging houses where a berth or " bunk" —one out of fifty in the same room—might be had for $6 a week.

The model of these establishments—which were far from being " model lodging-houses"—was that of a ship. A number of state-rooms, containing six berths each, ran around the sides of a large room, or cabin, where the lodgers resorted to read, write, smoke and drink at their leisure. The state-rooms were consequently filled with foul and unwholesome air, and the noises in the cabin prevented the passengers from sleeping, except between midnight and four o'clock.

The great want of San Francisco was society. Think of a city of thirty thousand inhabitants, peopled by men alone ! The like of this was never seen before. Every man was his own housekeeper, doing, in many instances, his own sweeping, cooking, washing and mending. Many home-arts, learned rather by observation than experience, came conveniently into play. He who cannot make a bed, cook a beefsteak, or sew up his own rips and rents, is unfit to be a citizen of California. Nevertheless, since the town began to assume a permanent shape, very many of the comforts of life in the East were attainable. A family may now live there without suffering any material privations ; and if every married man, who intends spending some time in California, would take his family with him, a social influence would soon be created to which we might look for the happiest results.

Towards the close of my stay, the city was as dismal a place as could well be imagined. The glimpse of bright, warm, serene weather passed away, leaving in its stead a raw, cheerless, south-east storm. The wind now and then blew a heavy gale, and the cold, steady fall of rain, was varied by claps of thunder and sudden blasts of hail. The mud in the streets became little short of fathomless, and it was with difficulty that the mules could drag their empty wagons through. A powerful London dray-horse, a very giant in harness, was the only animal able to pull a good load ; and I was told that he earned his master $100 daily. I saw occasionally a company of Chinese workmen, carrying bricks and mortar, slung by ropes to long bamboo poles. The plank side-walks, in the lower part of the city, ran along the brink of pools and quicksands, which the Street Inspector and his men vainly en-deavored to fill by hauling cart-loads of chapparal and throwing sand on the top ; in a day or two the gulf was as deep as ever. The side-walks, which were made at the cost of $5 per foot, bridged over the worst spots, but I was frequently obliged to go the whole length of a block in order to get on the other side. One could not walk any distance, without getting at least ancle-deep, and although the thermometer rarely sank below 50°, it was impossible to stand still for even a short time without a death-like chill taking hold of the feet. As a consequence of this, coughs and bronchial affections were innumerable. The universal custom of wearing the pantaloons inside the boots threatened to restore the knee-breeches of our grandfathers' times. Even women were obliged to shorten their skirts, and wear high-topped boots. The population seemed to be composed entirely of dismounted hussars. All this will be remedied when the city is two years older, and Portsmouth Square boasts a pavé as elegant as that on the dollar side of Broadway.

The severe weather occasioned a great deal of sickness, espe-cially among those who led an exposed life. The city overflowed with people, and notwithstanding buildings were continually grow-ing up like mushrooms, over night, hundreds who arrived were obliged to lodge in tents, with which the summits of the hills were covered. Fever-and-ague and dysentery were the prevailing com-plaints, the great prevalence of which was owing undoubtedly to

exposure and an irregular habit of life. An association was formed to relieve those in actual want, many of the wealthiest and
most influential citizens taking an honorable part in the matter.
Many instances of lamentable destitution were by this means
brought to light. Nearly all the hospitals of the place were soon
filled, and numbers went to the Sandwich Islands to recruit. The
City Hospital, a large, well ventilated and regulated establishment, contained about fifty patients. The attending physician
described to me several cases of nearly hopeless lunacy which had
come under his care, some of them produced by disappointment
and ill-luck, and others by sudden increase of fortune. Poor
human nature!

In the midst of the rains, we were greeted one morning with a
magnificent spectacle. The wind had blown furiously during the
night, with violent falls of rain, but the sun rose in a spotless sky,
revealing the Coast Mountains across the bay wrapped in snow
half-way down their sides. For two days they wore their dazzling
crown, which could be seen melting away hour by hour, from their
ridges and cloven ravines. This was the only snow I saw while in
San Francisco; only once did I notice any appearance of frost.
The grass was green and vigorous, and some of the more hardy
plants in blossom; vegetables, it is well known, flourish with equal
luxuriance during the winter season. At one of the restaurants,
I was shown some remarkable specimens of the growth of California soil—potatoes, weighing from one to five pounds each; beets
and turnips eight inches in diameter, and perfectly sweet and
sound; and large, silver-skinned onions, whose delicate flavor the
most inveterate enemy of this honest vegetable could not but have
relished. A gentleman who visited the port of Bodega, informed
me that he saw in the garden of Capt. Smith, the owner of the

place, pea-vines which had produced their third crop from the
same root in one summer.

As the rains drove the deer and other animals down from the
mountains, game of all kinds became abundant. Fat elks and
splendid black-tailed does hung at the doors of all the butcher-
shops, and wild geese, duck and brant, were brought into the
city by the wagon-load. " Grizzly bear steak," became a choice
dish at the eating-houses ; I had the satisfaction one night of
eating a slice of one that had weighed eleven hundred pounds.
The flesh was of a bright red color, very solid, sweet, and nutritious; its flavor was preferable to that of the best pork. The
large native hare, a specimen of which occasionally found its way
to the restaurants, is nowise inferior to that of Europe. As an
illustration of the money which might be spent in procuring a
meal no better than an ordinary hotel-dinner at home, I may
mention that a dinner for fifteen persons, to which I was invited,
at the " Excelsior," cost the giver of it $225.

The effect of a growing prosperity and some little taste of luxury
was readily seen in the appearance of the business community of
San Francisco. The slouched felt hats gave way to narrow-brim-
med black beavers; flannel shirts were laid aside, and white
linen, though indifferently washed, appeared instead; dress and
frock coats, of the fashion of the previous year in the Atlantic
side, came forth from trunks and sea-chests; in short, a San
Francisco merchant was almost as smooth and spruce in his outward appearance as a merchant anywhere else. The hussar
boot, however, was obliged to be worn, and a variation of the
Mexican sombrero—a very convenient and becoming head-piece—
came into fashion among the younger class.

The steamers which arrived at this time, brought large quantities of newspapers from all parts of the Atlantic States. The speculation which had been so successful at first, was completely overdone ; there was a glut in the market, in consequence whereof newspapers came down to fifty and twenty-five cents apiece. The leading journals of New-York, New-Orleans and Boston were cried at every street-corner. The two papers established in the place issued editions " for the Atlantic Coast," at the sailing of every steamer for Panama. The offices were invaded by crowds of purchasers, and the slow hand-presses in use could not keep pace with the demand. The profits of these journals were almost incredible, when contrasted with their size and the amount of their circulation. Neither of them failed to count their gains at the rate of $75,000 a year, clear profit.

My preparations for leaving San Francisco, were made with the regret that I could not remain longer and see more of the wonderful growth of the Empire of the West. Yet I was fortunate in witnessing the most peculiar and interesting stages of its progress, and I took my departure in the hope of returning at some future day to view the completion of these magnificent beginnings. The world's history has no page so marvellous as that which has just been turned in California.

CHAPTER VII.

SOCIETY IN CALIFORNIA.

THERE are some features of Society in California, which I have hitherto failed to touch upon in my narrative, but which deserve a passing notice before I take my final leave of that wonderful land. The direct effect of the state of things growing out of the discovery of the placers, was to develop new qualities and traits of character, not in single individuals, but in every individual of the entire community—traits frequently most unlooked-for in those who exhibited them in the most marked degree. Society, therefore, was for the time cast into new forms, or, rather, deprived of any fixed form. A man, on coming to California, could no more expect to retain his old nature unchanged, than he could retain in his lungs the air he had inhaled on the Atlantic shore.

The most immediate and striking change which came upon the greater portion of the emigrants was an increase of activity, and proportionately, of reckless and daring spirit. It was curious to see how men hitherto noted for their prudence and caution took sudden leave of those qualities, to all appearance, yet only prospered the more thereby. Perhaps there was at bottom a vein of keen, shrewd calculation, which directed their seemingly heedless movements ; certain it is, at least, that for a long time the rashest speculators were the most fortunate. It was this fact, no doubt, that seemed so alarming to persons newly-arrived, and gave rise to unnumbered predictions of the speedy and ruinous crash of the whole business fabric of San Francisco. But nothing is more contagious than this spirit of daring and independent action, and the most doleful prophets were, ere long, swallowed up in the same whirlpool against which they had warned others.

The emigrants who arrive in California, very soon divide into two distinct classes. About two-thirds, or possibly three-fourths of them are active, hopeful and industrious. They feel this singular intoxication of society, and go to work at something, no matter what, by which they hope to thrive. The remaining portion see everything " through a glass, darkly." Their first bright anticipations are unrealized; the horrid winds of San Francisco during the dry season, chill and unnerve them : or, if they go to the placers, the severe labor and the ill success of inexperienced hands, completes their disgust. They commit a multitude of sins in the shape of curses upon every one who has written or spoken favorably of California. Some of them return home without having seen the country at all, and others, even if they obtain profitable situations, labor without a will. It is no place for a slow, an over-cautious, or a desponding man. The emigrant should be willing to work, not only at one business, but many, if need be ; the grumbler or the idler had far better stay at home.

It cannot be denied that the very activity of California society created a spirit of excitement which frequently led to dangerous excesses. The habits of the emigrants, never, even at home, very slow and deliberate, branched into all kinds of wild offshoots, the necessary effect of the sudden glow and expansion which they experienced Those who retained their health seemed to revel in an exuberance of animal spirits, which carried them with scarce a jar over barriers and obstacles that would have brought others to a full stand. There was something exceedingly hearty, cordial and encouraging in the character of social intercourse. The ordinary forms of courtesy were flung aside with a bluntness of good-fellowship infinitely preferable, under the circumstances. I was constantly reminded of the stories of Northern History—of the stout Vikings and Jarls who exulted in their very passions and made their heroes of those who were most jovial at the feast and most easily kindled with the rage of battle. Indeed, it required but little effort of the imagination to revive those iron ages, when the rugged gold-diggers, with their long hair and unshorn beards, were grouped around some mountain camp-fire, revelling in the ruddy light and giving full play to a mirth so powerful and profound that it would not have shamed the Berserkers.

The most common excesses into which the Californians run, are drinking and gambling. I say drinking, rather than drunkenness, for I saw very little of the latter. But a single case came under my observation while I was in the gold region. The man's friends took away his money and deposited it in the hands of the Alcalde, then tied him to a tree where they left him till he became sober. The practice of drinking, nevertheless, was widely prevalent, and its effects rendered more destructive by the large amount of bad liquor which was sent into the country. Gambling, in spite of a universal public sentiment against it, grew and flourished ; the disappointment and ruin of many emigrants were owing to its existence. The gamblers themselves were in many instances men who had led orderly and respectable lives at home. I have heard some of them frankly avow that nothing would induce them to acquaint their friends and families with the nature of their occupation ; they would soon have enough, they said, and then they would wash their hands of the unclean stain, and go home to lead more honorable lives. But alas ! it is not so easy to wash out the memory of self-degradation. If these men have in truth any sentiment of honor remaining, every coin of the wealth they have hoarded will awaken a shameful consciousness of the base and unmanly business by which it was obtained.

In spite, however, of all these dissipating and disorganizing influences, the main stock of society was sound, vigorous and progressive. The rank shoots, while they might have slightly weakened the trunk, only showed the abundant life of the root. In short, without wishing to be understood as apologizing in any degree for the evils which existed, it was evident that had the Californians been more cool, grave and deliberate in their temperament—had they lacked the fiery energy and impulsive spirit which pushed them irresistibly forward—the dangers which surrounded them at the outset would have been far more imminent. Besides, this energy did not run at random ; it was in the end directed by an enlightened experience, and that instinct of Right, which is the strength and security of a self-governed People. Hundreds of instances might be adduced to show that the worst passions of our nature were speedily developed in the air of California, but the one grand lesson of the settlement and organization of the country is of a character that ennobles the race.

The unanimity with which all united in this work—the frankness with which the old prejudices of sect and party were disclaimed—the freshly-awakened pride of country, which made every citizen jealously and disinterestedly anxious that she should acquit herself honorably in the eyes of the Nation at large—formed a spectacle which must claim our entire admiration. In view of the splendid future which is opening for California, it insures her a stable foundation on which to build the superstructure of her wealth and power.

After what has been said, it will appear natural that California should be the most democratic country in the world. The practical equality of all the members of a community, whatever might be the wealth, intelligence or profession of each, was never before thoroughly demonstrated. Dress was no guage of respectability, and no honest occupation, however menial in its character, affected a man's standing. Lawyers, physicians and ex-professors dug cellars, drove ox-teams, sawed wood and carried luggage; while men who had been Army privates, sailors, cooks or day laborers were at the head of profitable establishments and not infrequently assisted in some of the minor details of Government. A man who would consider his fellow beneath him, on account of his appearance or occupation, would have had some difficulty in living peaceably in California. The security of the country is owing, in no small degree, to this plain, practical development of what the French reverence as an abstraction, under the name of *Fraternité*. To sum up all in three words, LABOR IS RESPECTABLE: may it never be otherwise, while a grain of gold is left to glitter in Californian soil !

I have dwelt with the more earnestness on these features of Society because they do not seem to be fully appreciated on this side of the Continent. I cannot take leave, in the regular course of my narrative, of a land where I found so much in Nature to admire and enjoy, without attempting to give some general, though imperfect view of Man, as he appeared under those new and wonderful influences.

CHAPTER VIII.

THE rainy season, by rendering further travel very unsatisfactory and laborious, if not impossible, put an end to my wanderings in California, which, in fact, had already extended beyond the period I had originally fixed for my stay. I was therefore anxious to set out on my homeward journey through Mexico, to which I looked forward with glowing anticipations. Rather than wait for the steamer of Jan. 1st., I decided to take one of the sailing packets up for Mazatlan, as the trip down the coast is usually made in from ten to fifteen days. The most promising chance was that of a Peruvian brigantine belonging to a German house, which I was assured would sail on the 15th of December. A heavy gale coming up at the time put this out of the question. I waited until the 17th, when I went on board, determined to set foot no more in San Franciscan mud. The brigantine—which bore the name of Iquiqueña, from the Peruvian port of Iquiqua—was a small, rakish craft, built at the Island of Chiloë for a smuggler in the opium trade; having been afterwards purchased by a house in Callao, she still retained the Peruvian colors.

In her low, confined cabin, containing eight berths, which were reached by a dark and crooked well, opening on the deck near the

rudder, seven passengers were crowded—Americans, Mexicans and
Venezuelans—besides the captain, mate, supercargo and steward,
who were Germans, as were likewise the greater part of the crew.
To complete the circle that met around our little table to discuss
the invariable daily dinner of rice soup and boiled beef, I must
not omit mentioning a Chinese dog, as eccentric in his behavior
as the Celestials on shore. The captain and crew did nothing to
falsify the national reputation for tardiness and delay. In our
case the *poco tiempo* of the Chagres boatmen was outdone. Seven
days were we doomed to spend in the Bay, before the almost
hopeless conjunction of wind, tide, crew, passengers and vessel
started us from our anchorage. On getting aboard, the captain
declared everything to be in readiness, except the wood and water,
which would be forthcoming next day. Having some experience
of German deliberation, I at once resigned myself to three days'
delay. The next day was stormy and rough; on the second, two
casks of water were brought on board; the third was stormy; the
wood was purchased on the fourth; and on the fifth, the sailors
quarreled about their pay and refused to go to sea.

While we thus lay in the harbor, just inside the Rincon, trying
to bear with patience a delay so vexatious, one of the terrible
south-east gales came on. The wind gradually rose through the
night, and its violence was heard and felt in the whistle of the
rigging and the uneasy roll of our brigantine. When morning
dawned, the sky was as gray and cold as an arch of granite,
except towards the south-east, where a streak of dun light seemed
like the opening through which the whole fury of the blast was
poured upon the bay. The timbers of the shipping creaked as
they were tossed about by the lashed and driven waters; the rigging hummed and roared till the ropes were ready to snap with

the violence of their vibrations. There was little rain accompanying the gale, but every drop stung like a shot. Seen under a sky and through an atmosphere from which all sensation of light and warmth was gone, the town and hills of San Francisco appeared as if cast in bronze, so cold, dark, and severe were their outlines. The blackest thunder-gusts I ever saw, had nothing so savage and relentless in their expression. All day and night, having dragged our anchor and drifted on the shoals, we lay thumping heavily with every swell, while a large barque, with three anchors out, threatened to stave in our bows. Towards morning the rain increased, and in the same proportion the gale abated. During its prevalence five or six vessels were injured, and two or three entirely lost.

The sailors having been pacified, the supercargo taken on board, and the brig declared ready for sea, we were detained another day on account of the anchor sticking fast in the mud, and still another through lack of a favorable wind. Finally, on the eighth day after going on board, the brig was warped through the crowded vessels, and took the first of the ebb tide, with a light breeze, to run out of the harbor.

I went on deck, in the misty daybreak, to take a parting look at the town and its amphitheatric hills. As I turned my face shoreward, a little spark appeared through the fog. Suddenly it shot up into a spiry flame, and at the same instant I heard the sound of gongs, bells and trumpets, and the shouting of human voices. The calamity, predicted and dreaded so long in advance, that men ceased to think of it, had come at last—San Francisco was on fire! The blaze increased with fearful rapidity. In fifteen minutes, it had risen into a broad, flickering column, making all the shore, the misty air and the water ruddy as with another sunrise. The sides of new frame houses, scattered through the town, tents high up on the hills, and the hulls and listless sails of vessels in the bay, gleamed and sparkled in the thick atmosphere. Meanwhile the roar and tumult swelled, and above the clang of gongs and the cries of the populace, I could hear the crackling of blazing timbers, and the smothered sound of falling roofs. I climbed into the rigging and watched the progress of the confla- gration. As the flames leaped upon a new dwelling, there was a sudden whirl of their waving volumes—an embracing of the frail walls in their relentless clasp—and, a second afterwards, from roof and rafter and foundation-beam shot upward a jet of fire, steady and intense at first, but surging off into spiral folds and streamers, as the timbers were parted and fell.

For more than hour, while we were tacking in the channel between Yerba Buena Island and the anchorage, there was no apparent check to the flames. Before passing Fort Montgomery, however, we heard several explosions in quick succession, and conjectured that vigorous measures had been taken to prevent further destruction. When at last, with a fair breeze and bright sky, we were dashing past the rock of Alcatraz, the red column had sunk away to a smouldering blaze, and nothing but a heavy canopy of smoke remained to tell the extent of the conflagration. The Golden Gate was again before us, and I looked through its mountain-walls on the rolling Pacific, with full as pleasant an excitement as I had looked inwards, four months before, eager to catch the first glimpse of the new Eldorado.

The breeze freshened, the swell increased, and as the breakers of the entrance receded behind us, we entered the rough sea left by a recent gale. In trying to haul close to the wind, the captain discovered that the rudder was broken. Immediately afterwards, there was a cry of " a leak !" and from the terror on the faces of the mate and sailors, I thought that nothing less than a dozen blankets could stop the opening. The pumps were rigged in haste, but little water was found in the hold, and on examination it appeared that the leak, which was in the bow, was caused by the springing apart of the planking from a violent blow on the rocks, which the brig had received a short time previous. The captain decided at once to return, much to our disappointment, as the wind was fair for Mazatlan. We were twenty miles from the entrance, and after beating up until next morning found ourselves just as far off as ever. The wind continuing fair, the captain at length listened to us, and turned again towards Mazatlan. A change of wind again changed his mind, and all that day and the next we tacked back and forth—sometimes running out towards the Farellones, sometimes close under the lee of the Punta de Los Reyes, and again driven down the coast as far, on the other side of the entrance What our brig gained in tacking, she lost in leeway, and as the rudder hung by a single pintle, she minded her helm badly. On the afternoon of the third day we were becalmed, but drifted into the entrance of the Gate with the flood-tide, in company with fifteen vessels, that had been waiting outside. A light southern breeze springing up, enabled us to reach the anchorage west of Clark's Point in the night ; so that next morning, after landing on the beach and walking through a mile of deep mud, I was once more in San Francisco.

I hastened immediately to Portsmouth Square, the scene of the conflagration. All its eastern front, with the exception of the Delmonico Restaurant at the corner of Clay-st. was gone, together with the entire side of the block, on Washington-st. The Eldorado, Parker House, Denison's Exchange and the United States

Coffee House—forming, collectively, the great rendezvous of the city, where everybody could be found at some time of the day—were among the things that had been.   The fronts of the Verandah, Aguila de Oro, and other hells on Washington-st. were blackened and charred from the intense heat to which they were subjected, and from many of the buildings still hung the blankets by means of which they were saved.   Three days only had elapsed since the fire, yet in that time all the rubbish had been cleared away, and the frames of several houses were half raised.   All over the burnt space sounded one incessant tumult of hammers, axes and saws.   In one week after the fire, the Eldorado and Denison's Exchange stood completely roofed and weatherboarded, and would soon be ready for occupation.   The Parker House was to be re-built of brick, and the timbers of the basement floor were already laid.   The Exchange had been contracted for at $15,000, to be finished in two weeks, under penalty of forfeiting $150 for every additional day.   In three weeks from the date of the fire, it was calculated that all the buildings destroyed would be replaced by new ones, of better construction.   The loss by the conflagration was estimated at $1,500,000—an immense sum, when the number and character of the buildings destroyed, is considered.   This did not include the loss in a business way, which was probably $500,000 more.   The general business of the place, however, had not been injured.   The smaller gambling hells around and near Portsmouth Square were doing a good business, now that the head-quarters of the profession were destroyed.

Notwithstanding there was no air stirring at the time, the progress of the fire, as described by those who were on the spot, had something terrific in its character.   The canvas partitions of rooms shrivelled away like paper in the breath of the flames, and the dry, resinous wood of the outer walls radiated a heat so intense that houses at some distance were obliged to be kept wet to prevent their ignition. Nothing but the prompt measures of the city authorities and a plentiful supply of blankets in the adjacent stores, saved all the lower part of the city from being swept away. The houses in the path of the flames were either blown up or felled like trees, by cutting off the ground timbers with axes, and pulling over the structure with ropes fastened to the roof. The Spanish merchants on Washington street, and others living in adobe houses in the rear, were completely stupified by the danger, and refused to have their buildings blown up. No one listened to them, and five minutes afterwards, adobes, timbers and merchandize went into the air together.

A very few persons, out of the thousands present, did the work of arresting the flames. At the time of the most extreme danger, hundreds of idle spectators refused to lend a hand, unless they were paid enormous wages. One of the principal merchants, I was told, offered a dollar a bucket for water, and made use of several thousand buckets in saving his property. All the owners of property worked incessantly, and were aided by their friends, but at least five thousand spectators stood idle in the plaza. I hope their selfish indifference is not a necessary offshoot of society here. It is not to be disputed, however, that constant familiarity with the shifting of Fortune between her farthest extremes, blunts very much the sympathies of the popular heart.

The German house of whom I had obtained a passage for Mazatlan, was burned out, but the supercargo soon discovered its whereabouts. A committee of sea-captains, appointed to examine the brigantine, reported that she could be made ready for sea in three or four days. Under these circumstances, the owners refused to refund more than half the passage-money, which was $75, to those of us who chose to leave the vessel. My time was now growing precious, and I had no doubt the three days spoken of would be extended to as many weeks. I therefore went to the office of the Pacific Mail Steamship Company, where, as I expected, every ticket had been taken weeks before, and neither love, money nor entreaty seemed likely to procure one. Mr. Robinson, the Agent, however, with a prompt kindness I shall not soon forget, gave me a passage to Mazatlan, with the understanding that I would have no berth and probably little sleeping-room.

The steamer was to sail on the first of January, at daybreak. After coming upon my friends like an apparition—they having supposed me to be far out at sea—I spent two days on shore, housed up from rain and mud, and finally took a boat for the steamer on the last evening of the year 1849. It was during the prevalence of the spring-tides, and no boat could be had to go from the Long Wharf to the anchorage off the Rincon, for less than $4. I had two oarsmen for myself and blankets; it was near the middle of the ebb-tide, and we ran inside the shelter of the point till we were abreast of the steamer. She was now about three-quarters of a mile distant, but a foaming, raging flood was between us. Several large boats, manned by four and six oarsmen were struggling in the midst of the current, and borne away in spite of themselves. One of my men was discouraged, and wanted to turn back, but there was a majority against him. I took good hold of the tiller-ropes, the men stripped to their flannel shirts, planted their feet firmly against the ribs of the boat, and we dashed into the teeth of the tide. We were thrown and tossed about like a toy; the spray flew over us, and the strongest efforts of the men did not seem to move us an inch. After half an hour of hard work, during which we continually lost ground, we came alongside of a vessel and made fast. At least a dozen other craft could be seen struggling out after us, but they all fell away, some of them drifting two or three miles before they could make a halt. We lay for nearly two hours, waiting for the height of the ebb to pass, but the flood still foamed and rushed, dashing against the prows of vessels and boiling around their sterns, with an incessant roar. At last, another boat with two passengers came down upon us in the darkness; we joined crews, leaving one of the boats behind, and set out again with four oars. It was pitchy dark, with a rain dashing in our faces. We kept on, towards the light of the steamer, gaining about a yard a minute, till we reached her lee gangway.

I unrolled my blankets and put in a preëmption claim for one end of the cabin-table. Several other berthless persons occupied the benches on either hand and the iron grating below, which printed their sides like a checker-board; and so we passed the night. The last boat-loads came out in the morning; the parting gun echoed back from the Island of Yerba Buena; the paddles moved; San Francisco slid away from us, and the Golden Gate opened again; the swells of the Pacific rolled forward to meet us; the coast wheeled around and fronted our larboard side; rain and fog were behind us, and a speck of clear blue far ahead—and so we sped southward, to the tropics, and homeward!

The Oregon's freight, both of gold and passengers, was the most important which had ever left San Francisco. Of the former, we had about two millions of dollars on board; of the latter, the Congressmen and Senators elect, Col. Frémont, Dr. Gwin, Gilbert and Wright, together with a score of the prominent merchants and moneyed men of San Francisco, and several officers

of the Army and Navy. Mr. Butler King was returning from
his survey of the country; Major Rucker, whom I have already
mentioned in connection with the overland emigration, and Major
Cross, recently from Oregon, were also on board. The character
of our little community was very different from that which came
up on the Panama; the steamer was under better regulations, and
at meal-time, especially, there was no disgraceful exhibition of
(for want of a better word) swinishness, such as I witnessed on the
former boat. We had a mild and spring-like temperature during
the trip, and blue skies, after doubling Cape Conception.

We touched at Santa Barbara on the third morning out. The
night had been foggy, and we ran astray in the channel between
the Island of Santa Rosa and the mainland, making the coast about
twenty-five miles south of the town. I did not regret this, as it
gave me an opportunity of seeing the point where the Coast Mountains come down to the sea, forming a narrow pass, which can only
be traveled at low tide, between the precipice and the surf. It is
generally known as the Rincon, or Corner—a common Spanish
term for the jutting end of a mountain; in a Californian ballad
(written before seeing the country,) I had made it the scene of an
imaginary incident, giving the name of *Paso del Mar*—the Pass
of the Sea—to the spot. I was delighted to find so near a corre-
spondence between its crags of black rock, its breakers and reaches
of spray-wet sand, and the previous picture in my imagination.
The village of Santa Barbara is charmingly situated, on a warm
slope above the roadstead, down to which stretch its fields of wheat
and barley. Behind it, on a shelf of the mountain, stands the
Mission, or Episcopal Residence of Santa Barbara, its white
arched corridors and tall square towers brightly relieved against the
pine forests in the distance. Above and beyond all, the Moun-

tain of Santa Ynez lifts its bold and sterile ramparts, like an unscaleable barrier against the inland.

We lay-to in the road for several hours, shipping supplies. The shore was so near that we could watch the vaqueros, as they galloped among the herds and flung their lariats over the horns of the doomed beeves. An immense whale lay stranded on the beach like the hull of some unlucky vessel. As we steamed down the coast, in the afternoon, we had a magnificent view of the snowy range which divides the rich vine-land of Los Angeles from the Tulare Plains. At daybreak the next morning we were in the harbor of San Diego, which was little changed since my visit in August; the hills were somewhat greener, and there were a few more tents pitched around the hide-houses. Thence away and down the rugged Peninsula—past the Bay of Sebastian Viscaino, the headland of San Lorenzo and the white deserts of sand that stretch far inland—around the jagged pyramids and hollow caverns of Cape San Lucas—beyond the dioramic glimpse of San José, and into the mouth of the Californian Gulf, where we were struck aback by a norther that strained our vessel's sinews and troubled the stomachs of her passengers. The next morning we groped about in the fog, hearing a breaker here and seeing a rock there, but the captain at last hit upon the right clue and ran us out of the maze into a gush of dazzling sunshine and tropic heat, which lay upon the islands and palmy shores of Mazatlan Harbor.

CHAPTER IX.

MAZATLAN.

I took leave of my friends and mess-mates, receiving many gloomy predictions and warnings of danger from the most of them, and went ashore with the captain, in the ship's boat. The water is very shallow, from within a mile of the landing, and abounds with rocks which rise nearly to the surface. Two of these are called The Turtles, from an incident which is told at the expense of an officer of the British Navy. He had just reached Mazatlan, and on his first visit to the shore, knowing that the waters contained turtle, had provided himself with rope and harpoon, and took his station in the bow of the boat. The men rowed for some time without interruption, but suddenly, at a whisper from the officer, backed their oars and awaited the throw. The harpoon was swung quickly to give it impetus ; the water flew as it descended ; " hit !" shouted the officer. And it *was* hit—so hard that the harpoon banged back again from the round face of the rock.

We landed on the beach, where we were instantly surrounded with the peons of the Custom House, in white shirts and pantaloons. The baggage was carried under the portico of an adobe house opposite the landing, where it was watched by one of the officials. Mr. Mott, of Mazatlan, who came passenger in the Ore-

BAYARD TAYLOR.

MAZATLAN.

NEW YORK, GEO. P. PUTNAM.

LITH. OF SARONY & MAJOR N.Y.

gon, was well-known to all the authorities of the place, and I found, after losing much time in getting a permit to have my luggage passed, that it had all been sent to his house without examination. My next care was to find a lodging-place. There was the *méson*, a sort of native caravanserai; the *Ballo de Oro*, (Golden Ball,) a tavern after the Mexican fashion, which is comfortless enough; and finally the *Fonda de Canton*, a Chinese hotel, kept by Luën-Sing, one of the most portly and dignified of all the Celestials. His broad face, nearly equal in circumference to the gong which Chin-Ling, the waiter, beat three times a day at the door, beamed with a paternal regard for his customers. His oblique eyes, in spite of all their twinklings after the main chance, looked a good-natured content, and his capacious girth spoke too well of fat living to admit of a doubt about the quality of his table. There was no resisting the attractions of Luën-Sing's hotel, as advertised in his own person, and thither, accordingly, I went.

The place was overrun by our passengers, who nearly exhausted the supplies of eggs, milk and vegetables in the market. The Fonda de Canton was thronged; all the rooms were filled with tables, and gay groups, like children enjoying a holiday, were clustered in the palm-shaded court-yard. Chin-Ling could not half perform the commands; he was called from every side and scolded by everybody, but nothing could relax the gravity of his queer yellow face. The sun was intensely hot until near evening, and I made myself quite feverish by running after luggage, permits and passports. I was not sorry when the gun of the steamer, at dusk, signalized her departure, and I was left to the company and hospitalities of my friend Luën-Sing. After the monte players had closed their bank in one of the rooms and the customers had with-

drawn, Chin-Lıng carried in a small cot, and made me a very
good bed, on which I slept nearly as soundly as if it had been soft
plank.

I took a ramble about the city in the clear coolness of the morning. Its situation is very peculiar and beautiful. Built at the
foot of a bold hill, it stands on the neck of a rocky, volcanic headland,
fronting the sea on each side, so that part of the city looks up the
Californian Gulf and part down the coast towards San Blas. The
houses are stone, of a white, pink or cream-color, with heavy
arched entrances and cool court-yards within. The contrast of
their clear, bright fronts, with the feathery tops of the cocoa-palm,
seen under a dazzling sky, gives the city a rich oriental character,
reminding me of descriptions of Smyrna. The houses are mostly
a single story in height, but in the principal street there are several
magnificent buildings of two stories, with massive cornices and
large balconied windows. The streets are clean and cheerful, and
the principal shops are as large, showy and tastefully arranged as
those of Paris or New York. At night, especially, when they are
brilliantly lighted and all the doors and windows are opened, displaying the gaudy shawls, scarfs and sarapes within; when the
whole population is out to enjoy the pleasant air, the men in their
white shirts and the women in their bewitching rebosas; when
some native band is playing, just far enough distant to drown the
discordance; when the paper lanterns of the fruit-venders gleam
at every corner, and the aristocratic señoritas smoke their paper
cigars in the balconies above—Mazatlan is decidedly the gayest
and liveliest little city on the Continent.

But I was speaking of my morning stroll. The sun was already
shining hotly in the streets, and the mellow roar of the surf on the
northern side of the promontory tempted my steps in that direc-

tion. I threaded the narrow alleys in the suburbs of the town, lined with cactus hedges, behind which stood the thatched bamboo huts of the natives, exactly similar to those on the Isthmus. Gangs of men, naked to the waist, were at work, carrying on their heads large faggots of dye-wood, with which some of the vessels in the harbor were being freighted. I reached a shaded cove among the rocks, where I sat and looked out on the dark-blue expanse of the Gulf. The air was as transparent as crystal and the breakers rolled in with foam and delightful freshness, to bathe the shelly sand at my feet. Three craggy islands off the shore looked to be within gunshot, owing to the purity of the atmosphere, yet their scarred sides and ragged crests were clothed in the purple of distance. The region about the mouth of the Gulf of California enjoys an unvarying clearness of climate, to which there is probably no parallel on the earth. At Cape San Lucas, the rising and setting of a star is manifest to the naked eye. Two or three years frequently pass without a drop of rain. There is, however, a season of about a week's duration, occurring in some of the winter months, when the soil is kept continually moist from the atmosphere. Not a cloud is to be seen ; the sun is apparently as bright as ever ; yet a fine, gauzy film of moisture pervades the air, settles gradually on the surface of the earth and performs the service of rain.

I saw an interesting picture one evening, in front of the Theatre. A large band was stationed near the door, where they performed waltzes and polkas in excellent style—an idea no doubt derived from " Scudder's Balcony" or the gambling-hells of San Francisco. It had the effect, at least, to draw a dense crowd of the lower orders to the place, and increase the business of the traders in fruits and drinks. A military band, of trumpets alone, marched up and down the principal street, blowing long blasts of piercing sound that affected one like the shock of an electro-galvanic battery. Soldiers were grouped around the door of the Theatre, with stacked arms, and the tables of dealers in fruit and provisions were ranged along the walls. Over their braziers of charcoal simmered the pans of *manteca*, (lard,) near which stood piles of tortillas and dishes of fowl mixed with *chili colorado*, ready to be served up at a medio the plate. Bundles of sugar-cane were heaped upon the ground, and oranges, bananas, and other fruits spread upon mats beside which their owners sat. There were tables covered with porous earthern jars, containing cool and refreshing drinks made of orange juice, cocoa milk, barley flour, and other wholesome ingredients.

The market-place presents a most picturesque appearance, whether by day or night. It is a small square, on the steep side of the hill, reached by narrow alleys, in which are to be found all the articles most in demand by the lower classes—earthenware after the old Aztec fashion, flaming calicoes, sarapes, rebosas and broad Guayaquil sombreros. The place is filled with square, umbrella-like stands or canopies of palm-leaves, under which are spread on the ground all kinds of vegetables, fruit and grain that grow in the vicinity, to be had at low prices. Among the fruits I noticed a plump green berry, with a taste like a strawberry and gooseberry combined; they were called by the natives, *arellanes*. At night, the square was lighted by flaring lamps or torches of some resinous wood.

The proximity of California had increased in a striking manner the growth and activity of Mazatlan. Houses were going up in all parts of the towns, and the prices of articles in the shops were little below the San Francisco standard. At a tailoring establishment I was asked $20 for a pair of Mexican calzoneros, and $25 for a cloth traveling jacket—sums entirely above my reach. I purchased a good Panama hat for $5, and retaining my suit of corduroy and shirt of blue flannel, set about hunting for a mule. There were about fifty emigrants in the place, who had come in a few days previous, from Durango ; but their animals had all been disposed of to the Mexican traders, at very low prices. I was directed to the *méson*, where I found a number for sale, in the corral. The owners offered to sell me a *caballo sillado* (a saddled and bridled horse) for $100, or a tolerable mule for $80, but seemed to think I would prefer a *frisone*, (an American horse,) at $100, unsaddled. After riding a number of mules around the corral, I made choice of a small brown one, for which $45 was asked, but which I obtained for $30. One of the emigrants sold me his saddle and bridle for $5 ; I added a good lariat and blanket, and was thoroughly equipped for the journey.

It now remained to have my passport arranged, for which the signature of the President of the City Council was requisite. After a great deal of search, I found the proper place, where a sort of Alcalde, who was settling a dispute between two Indians, wrote a *visto*, and directed me to call on the President, Don Luis Abioli. This second visit cost me several hours, but at last I succeeded in discovering Don Luis, who was busily engaged behind the counter of his grocery store, in a little building near the market-place. He stopped weighing sugar to affix his signature to the passport, received my " *mil gracias !*" with a profound bow and turned again to his customers.

The emigrants expressed great astonishment at my fool-hardiness, as they termed it, in undertaking the journey through to Vera Cruz. These men, some of whom had come overland from

Chihuahua and some from Matamoras, insisted most strenuously that I should not start alone. The Mexicans, they said, were robbers, to a man ; one's life, even, was not safe among them, and their bitter hostility to Americans would subject me to continual insult. " Would you believe it ?" said a tall, raw-boned Yankee ; " they actually *rocked* us !" This gentle proceeding, I found, on further inquiry, had been occasioned by the emigrants breaking their contract with their guide. I therefore determined to follow the plan I had adopted in California, and to believe nothing that I had not seen with my own eyes. " I've traveled in the country, and I know all about it," was the remark with which I was constantly greeted ; " you'll very soon find that I was right." To escape from the annoyance of these counsels and warnings, I hastened my preparations, and was ready for departure on the second morning after my arrival.

Luën-Sing, who had traveled over the road once, as far as Tepic, told me I should find it toilsome but safe. The Celestials assisted me in packing my scanty luggage behind the saddle, and enjoined on me the promise of patronizing the *Fonda de Canton*, when I returned to Mazatlan. I took my final cup of chocolate on the old table in the corridor, had a last talk with Chin-Ling about the gold-diggings, shook hands with the whole yellow-faced, long-eyed crew, mounted my mule and started up the main street, in the breathless heat of a noonday sun. I doubled the corner of the hill, passing the *Plaza de Toros*, (an arena for bull-fights,) and the scattering huts of the suburbs, till I reached the *garita*, near the sea. Here, an officer of the customs, who was lounging in the shade, pointed out the road to the old Presidio of Mazatlan, which I took, feeling very warm, very lonely and a little dispirited at the ride of twelve hundred miles which lay before me.

CHAPTER X.

It was a cloudless noon. The sun burned down on the sand and quivering sea, and the three islands in the Gulf seemed vitrifying in the blue heat of the air. Riding slowly down to the arid level of a dried-up marsh, over which my path lay, I met an arriero, of whom I asked the distance to the Presidio. *" No llega hoy,"* said he ; *" la mula no anda nada ; es muy flojo."* (You'll not get there to-day ; your mule don't go at all ; " he's very lazy.") My heart misgave me for a moment, for his criticism of the mule was true ; but, seeing that my spur had as yet drawn no blood, I broke a stick from the thicket and belabored him with hand and foot. I passed a few plantations, with fenced fields, near the town, and afterwards took to the sandy chapparal near the sea.

The foliage of a tropical winter, on this coast, is not very attractive. There is a season when the growth is suspended—when the bud closes, the leaf falls and the bough gathers sap for a long time of splendid bloom. Only the glossy green of the lemon, mango and sycamore remains ; the rest of the wood takes a grayish cast from its many half-clothed boughs, among which rise the strange, gloomy pillars of the *cereus giganteus,* often more than forty feet in height. After making the circuit of a spacious bay, I came to a cluster of fishing huts on the shore, about three leagues from Mazatlan. Beyond these the road turned among low hills, covered with the gray, wintry woods, as far as eye could reach. Gaudy parrots flew screaming among the boughs ; large brown birds, with hooked bills sat musing by the road, and in the shady spots, I heard the tender coo of the dove—the sweet emblem of peace and domestic affection, to which no clime is alien—which haunts all lands and all zones, where beats the human heart whose softer emotions it typifies.

I was toiling along in the heat, torturing my conscience as much as the mule's flanks, when a couple of rancheros, riding behind me, came up with a good-humored greeting and proposed joining company. The foremost, a merry old native, of mixed blood, commenced using his whip on my mule's back and I soon found that the latter could keep up a sharp trot for an hour, without trouble. Thanks to my self-constituted *mozo*, I reached the banks of the Rio Mazatlan, opposite the Presidio, two hours before sunset. The old man invited me to pass the night at his ranche, which was near to hand, and I willingly complied. He turned his own beast loose, and started to a neighboring ranche, for an armful of *oja* (the fodder of maize) for my mule. Meanwhile, I walked down to the river, to refresh myself with a bath. The beauty of the scene kept me from the water for a long time. On the opposite bank the old walls of the Presidio towered above the trees ; the valley, stretching away to the eastward, to a far-off line of mountains, out of a notch in which the river found its way, was spotted with plantations of maize, bananas and melons. The rancheros were out at work, ploughing and sowing their grain. The fervor of the day was over, and a warm, tempered light was poured over the landscape. As I lay, clasped in the

soft-flowing crystal of the river, the thought of another bath, on
that very day four years before, came suddenly into my mind. It
was my birth-day; but on that other anniversary I had baptized
my limbs in the sparkling surf of the Mediterranean, on the shore
of the Roman Campagna. I went back to the ranche with that
sensation of half-pain, half-joy, which we feel when the mind and
body are in different places.

My mule was fed and the old man gave me a dish of frijoles,
with three tortillas in lieu of knife and fork. Then we sat down
in the delicious twilight, amid the beautiful repose of Nature, and
I answered, as well as I could, the questions prompted by their
simple curiosity. I told them about my country and its climate,
aad the long journey I must yet make to reach it, which they
heard with evident interest and wonder. They were anxious to
know how a steamboat could move against the wind, for they had
been told this was the case, by their friends in Mazatlan. The
nearest idea of it which I could give them, was by describing it as
a *sea-cart*, with broad wheels rolling on the water. At last the
twilight deepened into night, and I unrolled my blankets to make
my bed. " You must sleep to-night *en el seréno*," said the old
man ; and a beautiful, star-lit *Seréno* it was. " Ah," said his
wife, " what fine blankets ! you will sleep better than the Arch-
bishop !" They then went to their hammocks in the hut, and I
lay down on the earth, thanking God that the dismal forebodings
which accompanied me out of Mazatlan had been so happily falsified.

My kind host asked nothing in payment, when I saddled in the
morning, but I insisted on giving him a trifle. " *Vaya con
Dios !*" said he, as we shook hands, " and if you go to California,
bring me a little piece of gold when you come back." I forded

the river and passed through old Mazatlan—a miserable village
of huts with a massive presidio and church in ruins. The morning was fresh and cool, and the road lay in shade for several
miles. My mule, having no whip behind him, was as lazy as ever
and made me the subject of remark from all the natives who
passed. A ranchero, carrying an escopette and three live turkeys
slung to the saddle, before him, offered his horse in exchange. I
refused to trade, but an hour later, met an arriero, with a train of
horses, laden with *oja*. He made the same proposition and un-
loaded the mountainous stack under which one of his horses was
buried, that I might try him. *"Es muy caminador,"* (a great
traveler,) said the owner ; but he was crooked-legged, sore-backed
and terribly thin in withers and flanks. Looking at him in front,
he seemed to have no breadth ; he was like a horse carved out of
plank, and I was almost afraid to mount, for fear I should pull
him over. Nevertheless, he started off briskly ; so without wast-
ing words, I made an even exchange. Nothing was gained
however, in point of dignity, for my brisk lean horse occasioned
quite as many remarks as my fat lazy mule.

Towards noon I reached a little village called Santa Fe, where
I got a breakfast of frijoles and chopped sausage, mixed with red-
pepper—a dish called *chorisa*—for a real. The country I passed
was hilly and barren, with a range of broken mountains between
me and the sea. Crossing a ridge beyond Santa Fe, I came upon
extensive fields of aloes, cultivated for the vinous drink called
mescal, which is made of their juice. In the midst of them stood
the adobe town of Agua Caliente—a neat though scattering place,
with a spacious church. I journeyed on for leagues in the burning sun, over scorched hills, without water or refreshing verdure.
My *caminador*, too, lost the little spirit he had displayed, and

jögged along at a snail's pace. I suffered greatly from thirst for several hours, till I reached a broad arroyo crossing the road, where I found a little muddy water at the bottom of a hole. Some Indians who were seated in the shade, near a sort of camp-fire, put me on the right trail for Potrerillos, the village where I expected to pass the night. A pleasantly shaded path of a league took me thither by sunset.

Mr. Brown—my old friend on the Rio Mazatlan told me I could stop wherever I chose, on the road; no ranchero would refuse to receive me. I accordingly rode up to the first house, and inquired; "Can I stay here to-night?" "Si Señor," was the ready answer. The place was small, and the people appeared impoverished, so I asked whether there was a posada in the place. "Go to Don Ipolito," said the man; "that is where the estranjeros stay," Don Ipolito was a Frenchman, who had an adobe hut and corral for mules, in the centre of the village. He was about starting for Mazatlan, but gave directions to the women and mozos to furnish me with supper, and my horse with corn and oja. His instructions were promptly obeyed; I had a table set with chorisa and frijoles, under the thatched portico; then a cup of black coffee and a puro, which I enjoyed together, while trying to comprehend the talk of a very pretty girl of fifteen and a handsome young ranchero, evidently her lover, who sat near me on a low adobe wall. They were speaking of marriage—that I found at once; but another ranchero—perhaps a rival suitor—named Pio, formed their principal topic. "Es sin verguënza, Pio" (He's a shameless fellow, that Pio,) was frequently repeated by both of them.

My bed-time was not long in coming. A boy was sent into the loft of the hut for a frame made of woven cane, which was placed

on the portico, and covered with a coarse matting. I threw my
blankets on it, using my coat for a pillow, and was sound asleep
in five minutes. Half an hour might have elapsed, when I was
suddenly aroused by a sound like the scream of a hundred fiends.
The frame on which I lay was rocked to and fro, and came near
overturning; I sprang up in alarm, finding my bed in the midst of
a black, moving mass, from which came the horrid sound. It
proved to be a legion of hogs, who had scented out a few grains of
corn in a basket which had held my horse's feed, and was placed
under the bed. The door of the hut opened, and the hostess appeared with a lamp. At sight of her, the beasts gave a hasty
grunt, cleared the wall at one bound, and disappeared. "Santa
Maria!" shrieked the woman; "son demonios—son hijos del
diablo!" (they are demons—they are children of the devil!) I
feared that another descent upon me would be made after she had
gone back to her hammock; but I was not molested again.

I arose in the morning, fed my horse, saddled, and was off by
sunrise. The town of El Rosario was but four leagues distant,
and the road was full of young rancheros in their holiday dresses,
riding thither to mass. Three of them joined company with me,
and tried to sell me one of their horses. "You'll never reach
Tepic with that horse," said they, "look at ours!" and away
they would gallop for a hundred yards, stopping with one bound,
to wait for my slow-paced caminador. They drew out their
tobacco and tinder-boxes, as we rode along; one of them, a spruce
young fellow, with a green silk sash around his waist, rolled his
cigarito in corn-husk, smoked about one-third of it and presented
me with the remainder, that I might see how much better it
tasted than paper. The flavor was indeed mild and delightful; I
puffed away an inch of it, and then returned him the stump. A

naked boy, basking in the sun at the door of a hut, called out
" *Yanki!* " as I passed.

El Rosario is built on a beautiful site, in a broad valley, surrounded by blue and jagged peaks. It has several streets of
spacious stone houses, for the most part ruined, and a church with
a fine stone tower a hundred and fifty feet in height. I had to
cross the plaza, which was filled with the rancheros of the neighborhood, waiting for the hour of mass ; my caminador was the
subject of general notice, and I was truly rejoiced when I had
hidden his raw bones from sight in the court-yard of a *fonda*.
The house was kept by a good-natured old lady, and three large
parrots, who, (the parrots) sat each on a different perch, continually repeating : " *chiquito perriquito, bonito, blanquito* !"—the
only phrase I ever heard a Mexican parrot utter, and which may
be thus translated : " very little, pretty little, white-little par-
rotling !" I ate my breakfast of beans and red-peppers, chatting
the while with the old lady, who was loud in her praises of Tepic,
whither I told her I was bound.   " *Es mi pais*," said she, " *es un
pais precioso*." She scolded me good-humoredly at starting, for
having left my horse where he might have been stolen, and bade
me beware of the robbers ; but, thought I, who would take such a
horse ?

Crossing the river of Rosario, I took a path embowered in green
thickets, through which glided multitudes of macaws and tufted
birds of gay plumage.   At noon I came into a lovely valley among
the mountains, and followed a stream shaded by splendid syca-
mores and palms.   Little patches of meadow land slept like still
lakes among the woods, with thatched ranches spotting their
shores.   I rode up to one of these for a drink of water, which an
old man brought me in a calabash, standing bare-headed till I had

finished drinking. The trails soon after scattered, and I found
that I had lost the main road. In this emergency I met a ranchero, who told me I had wandered far from the right track, but
that he would act as guide. I promised him a reward, if he would
accompany me, whereupon he ran to his hut for a lariat, caught a
horse and sprang on his unsaddled back. We rode for more than
two hours in a foot-path through the depths of the tangled forest,
before striking the road. The impervious screen of foliage above
our heads kept off the sun and turned the daylight into an emerald
gloom. Taking leave of my guide, I emerged from these lonely
and enchanting shades upon the burnt upland, where the tall fan-
palms rustled drearily in the hot wind. As the afternoon wore
away, another green level of billowy foliage appeared ahead ; the
hills lay behind me, and far away to the right I saw the sea-blink
along the edges of the sky.

Notwithstanding the unsurpassed fertility of soil and genial
character of climate, this region is very scantily settled, except in
the broad river-bottoms opening towards the sea. There, under
the influence of a perpetual summer, the native race becomes indolent and careless of the future. Nature does everything for
them ; a small patch of soil will produce enough maize and bananas
for a family, with which, and the eternal frijoles, they have abundance for life's wants. The saplings of the woods furnish them
with posts, rafters and ridge-poles, the palm and the cane with
thatch and bedding. They are exempt from all trouble as to
their subsistence ; the blue ramparts of the Sierra Madre on one
side, and the silver streak of the sea on the other, enclose their
world. They grow up lithe and agile in the free air, mate, wax
old and die, making never a step out of the blind though contented
round which their fathers walked before them. I do not believe

that a more docile or kindly-disposed people exists than these rancheros. In all my intercourse with them I was treated with unvarying honesty, and with a hospitality as sincere as it was courteous and respectful. During all my travels in the Tierra Caliente, I was never imposed upon as a stranger nor insulted as an American.

My resting-place the third night was the village of Escuinapa, where I found a *méson*, kept, or at least managed by a lady whose kindness and cheerfulness were exactly in proportion to her size ; that is, they were about as broad as they were long. She was a fast friend of the Americans, and spoke with rapture of the promptness with which all the emigrants whom she had entertained, had paid their bills. Her own countrymen, she said, were slippery customers; they frequently ran off without paying a *claco*. She talked of going to California ; she thought if she were to establish a *méson* in the diggings, all the emigrants who had passed through Escuinapa would patronize her. "They are all good people," said she ; "I like them as well as if they were my brothers, and I am sure they would come to visit me." An old man, who seemed to be her husband, sat swinging in the hammock, lifting his feet high enough that his blue velvet calzoneros should not be soiled on the floor. I had an excellent dinner of eggs, fish and chocolate, finishing with a delicate *cigarito* which the corpulent hostess prepared for me. Two or three Mexican travelers arrived for the night and took possession of the cane bed-frame and benches in the room, leaving me only the cold adobe floor. "Will you take out your saddle and bridle ?" requested the old lady ; "*los señores* are going to sleep here." "But where am I to sleep ?" I asked. "*Con migo !*" was the immediate answer. "*Como ?*" said I, surprised and alarmed ; I was horror-struck and must have looked

so, for she seemed amused at my bewilderment. " Come !" she
replied, and took up the lamp. I shouldered the saddle, and followed to a dark, windowless closet, in the rear of the house. It
was just large enough to hold two frames, covered with matting,
and some bags of maize and barley. " This is your bed," said she,
pointing to one of them, " and this is ours. I hope you do not
object to our sleeping in the same room." I laid my saddle on
the frame indicated, put my head on it, and slept soundly till the
early dawn shone through the cracks of the door.

Leaving Escuinapa, a day's journey of fifty miles lay before me,
through an uninhabited country. I doubted the powers of my
caminador, but determined to let him have a fair trial , so I gave
him a good feed of corn, drank a cup of chocolate, slung a pine-
apple to my saddle-bow, and rode out of the village in the morning
dusk. At first the trail led through pleasant woods, with here and
there a ranche, but diverging more and more to the east, it finally
came out on a sandy plain bordering the leagues of salt marsh on
the side towards the sea. On the left the mountain chain of the
Sierra Madre rose high and abrupt, showing in its natural but-
tresses and ramparts of rock a strong resemblance to the peaks of
the Gila country. A spur of the chain ran out towards the sea,
far in front, like the headland of a bay. The wide extent of salt
marsh reaching from near El Rosario to La Bayona—a distance
of seventy-five miles, showed the same recession of the Pacific, as
I had already observed at Panama and Monterey. The ancient
sea-margins may still be traced along the foot of the mountains.

I jogged steadily onward from sunrise till blazing noon, when,
having accomplished about half the journey, I stopped under a
palm-tree and let my horse crop a little grass, while I refreshed
myself with the pine-apple. Not far off there was a single ranche,

called Piedra Gorda—a forlorn-looking place, where one cannot remain long without being tortured by the sand-flies. Beyond it, there is a natural dome of rock, twice the size of St. Peters, capping an isolated mountain. The broad intervals of meadow between the wastes of sand were covered with groves of the beautiful fan-palm, lifting their tufted tops against the pale violet of the distant mountains. In lightness, grace and exquisite symmetry, the Palm is a perfect type of the rare and sensuous expression of Beauty in the South. The first sight of the tree had nearly charmed me into disloyalty to my native Pine ; but when the wind blew, and I heard the sharp, dry, metallic rustle of its leaves, I retained the old allegiance. The truest interpreter of Beauty is in the voice, and no tree has a voice like the Pine, modulated to a rythmic accord with the subtlest flow of Fancy, touched with a human sympathy for the expression of Hope and Love and Sorrow, and sounding in an awful undertone, to the darkest excess of Passion.

Making the circuit of the bay, the road finally doubled the last mountain-cape, and plunged into dark green thickets, fragrant with blossoms. I pushed on hour after hour, the pace of my caminador gradually becoming slower, and sunset approached without any sign of "Bayona's hold." Two Indians, mounted on small horses, came down by a winding trail from the hills, and rode a little in advance of me. " *No tiene uste miedo de viajar solo* ?" (Are you not afraid to travel alone ?) said one of them. " What should I be afraid of ?" I asked in return. " The robbers." " I should like to see them ;" I said. " *Tiene mucho valor,*" remarked one to the other. They then spoke of my tired horse, and looked admiringly at my blankets, asking me first to make a gift of them, then to sell them, and, finally, to let them carry them behind their own saddles. I refused them very decidedly, and they trotted in advance. At the next bend of the road, however, I saw through the trees that they waited till I nearly overtook them, when they slowly moved forward. The repetition of this roused my suspicions; taking off a heavy pair of gloves, I pulled out my pistol, put on a fresh cap, and kept it in my right hand. I believe they must have been watching my motions, for instead of waiting as usual, they dashed off suddenly at a gallop.

The sun went down ; the twilight faded, and the column of the zodiacal light shortened to the horizon, as I walked behind my caminador, looking for La Bayona. At last I came to a river, with two or three ranches on its banks; in front of them was a large fire, with several men standing about it. One of them offered to accompany me to the town, which was near. On the way, he expatiated on the great number of rabbits in the neighborhood, and lamented that he had no powder to shoot them, winding up with : " Perhaps, Señor, you might give me a little ; you can easily buy more when you reach Acaponeta." I poured out half the contents of my flask into a corner of his shirt, which he held up to receive it; he then pointed out the fording-place, and I crossed to La Bayona, where my poor horse had rest and good feed after his hard day's journey. There was a dirty little *méson* in the place, a bare room. In which was given me for two reales, and a supper of tortillas and frijoles for a medio (6¼ cents.)

The landlord and one of his friends talked with me a long while about the United States. " Tell me," said the latter, " is it true what Don Carlos, an American that was here last spring, told me—that there is a machine in your country in which you look at the moon, and it seems to be twenty feet long?" I assured him it was perfectly true, for I had often seen the moon

in it. "Is it also true," he continued, "that in the United
States a man pays only one dollar a year, and sends all his children to school for nothing?—and, then, when they have gone
twelve years to school, they are fit for any business? Ah, how
grand that is! how much better than here! Now, I do not
know how to read at all. Why is it that everything is so fortunate
in the United States?" "Because," said the other, "it is a
nation *muy poderosa.*" "I have heard that there are several
millions of people in it." "That is true," rejoined the other,
"and that is the reason why all the Americans we see are so much
wiser than we are." I was deeply interested in their naïve
remarks. In fact, not only here, but throughout all western
Mexico, I found none of the hostility to Americans which had
been predicted for me, but on the reverse, a decided partiality.
In speaking of us, the natives exhibited (and I say it not with any
feeling of national pride,) the liking which men bear to their
superiors. They acknowledged our greater power and intelligence
as a nation, without jealousy, and with an anticipation rather than
a fear, that our rule will one day be extended over them.

The next morning I rode to Acaponeta, four leagues distant, by
a pleasant road over low hills. The scenery was highly picturesque;
the town lies in the lap of a wide valley, nearly encircled by mountains which rise one above another, the farthest still the highest,
like the seats in an amphitheatre. Their sides are cloven by
tremendous chasms and ravines, whose gloom is concealed by perpetual verdure, but the walls of white rock, dropping sheer down
many hundreds of feet from the summit, stand out distinctly in
the vaporless atmosphere. Except the church and a few low
adobe buildings around the plaza, Acaponeta is formed entirely of
cane huts. I stopped at the *Meson del Angel*, gave a basket of

corn to my horse, and ordered eggs, beefsteak, and chocolate for breakfast. The *cocinera* and her daughter were two hours in preparing it, and meanwhile I sat in the shade of an orange tree, be- side a cool well in the court-yard. The women were very talka- tive, and amused themselves greatly with my bad Spanish. The daughter was preparing a quantity of empty egg-shells for the Carnival, by filling them with finely-minced paper of different colors and sealing the ends again. In order to show me how these were used, they bade me take off my hat. Each then took an egg and approached me, saying, " *tu es mi bien amorado*,"— at the same time breaking the shells on my head. My hair was completely filled with their many-colored contents, and it was several days before it was clear of this testimony of affection.

I crossed another large river at Acaponeta, and went on through embowered paths,

> " Under a shade perpetual, which never
> Ray of the sun let in, nor moon.

Gay parrots and macaws glanced in and out amid the cool green shawdows ; lovely vistas opened between the boughs into the faery heart of the wilderness ; the trees were laced each to each, by vines each more luxuriant than themselves ; subtile odors pervaded the air, and large, yellow, bell-shaped flowers swung on their long stems like cups of gold, tremulous in the chance rays of sunshine. Here and there, along the ledges of the mural mountains on my left, I noted the smoke of Indian camp-fires, which, as night ap- proached, sparkled like beacons. I intended to have stopped at a ranche called San Miguel, but passed it unknowingly, and night found me on the road. A friendly ranchero pointed out to me a path which led to a hut, but I soon lost it, and wandered

about at random on the dark fenceless meadows. At last I heard
a dog's bark—the sure sign of habitation—and, following the
sound, came to a small ranche.

I was at once given permission to stay, and the women went to
work on the tortillas for my supper. I swung off my fatigue in a
hammock, and supped by starlight on the food of the Aztecs—the
everlasting tortilla, which is a most nourishing and palatable cake
when eaten fresh from the hot stone on which it is baked. There
were several dogs about the ranche, and the biggest of them
showed a relentless hostility towards me. "El Chucho don't like
you," said the ranchero; "he'll bite if he can get hold of you;
you had better climb up there and sleep," and he pointed to a
sort of cane platform used for drying fruit, and raised on poles
about twelve feet from the ground. I took my blankets, climbed
up to the frail couch, and lay down under the stars, with Taurus
at the zenith. El Chucho took his station below; as often as I
turned on my airy bed during the night, the vile beast set up his
howl and all the dog-herd howled in concert.

The next day I breakfasted at the hacienda of Buena Vista and
rode about six leagues further, to the town of Rosa Morada. (The
Violet Rose.) Just before reaching the place I caught sight of a
mountain very far to the south, and recognized its outline as that
of the *Silla de San Juan* (Saddle of St. John,) which rises behind the roadstead of San Blas. This was a welcome sight,
for it marked the first step of my ascent to the Table-Land. I
was growing tired of the Tierra Caliente; my face was blistered
with the heat, and my skin so punctured by musquitos, fleas, sand-
flies and venomous bugs that I resembled a patient in the last
stage of small-pox. There was no *méson* in Rosa Morada, but a
miserable *posada*, where I found three Frenchmen, two of whom

were fresh from Bordeaux and on their way to California. They
were all engaged about the kitchen fire, concocting their dinner,
which they invited me to share with them. The materials they
picked up in the village were not slighted in the cooking, for
better vermicelli I never ate. They likewise carried their beds
with them and stretched their cot-frames on the airy portico. I
lay down on the adobes and slept "like a brick."

I was off at daylight, riding over an elevated plain towards the
Rio Santiago. Two arrieros, on their way to Tepic, shared their
tortillas with me and proposed we should join company. They
stopped two hours to noon, however, and I left them. Urging
forward my despairing horse, I crossed one branch of the river at
San Pedro and reached Santiago, on the main branch, an hour before sunset. In descending to the Rio Santiago—or, more properly, the Rio Tololotlan, its ancient Aztec apellation—I came
upon plantations of bananas and plantains, heavy with ripening
fruit. The country showed signs of wealth and culture; the
houses were large and well built and the fields divided by strong
fences of palm logs. All up and down the broad banks of the
river were scattered arrieros, mules and rows of pack-saddles,
while half a dozen large canoes were plying backwards and for-
wards with their loads. I got into the first vacant one with my
saddle, bridle and blankets, taking a turn of the lariat round my
horse's nose. An arriero who had passed me the day previous,
with a horse as worn-out as my own, was the other passenger.
The river is about sixty yards wide, and very deep and swift. Our
horses swam bravely behind us, and I believe were much the better for the bath.

I took an instant liking to the arriero for two reasons : firstly,
he had a dark, melancholy, intellectual eye ; secondly, he was the

only traveler I saw on the road, whose horse was so woeful an animal as mine. We started in company, and soon grew strongly attached. At dusk, we reached a village called Las Verritas. The inhabitants were all gone to Tepic, except an old man and a little boy who were selling *oja* to a company of muleteers squatted around a fire in the middle of the street. Nothing was to be had to eat, except some cheeses which one of the latter carried in a wicker pack. I could get no tortillas for money, nor exactly for love, but compassion helped me. The wife of one of the men came quietly to me as I sat by my saddle, and slipping two tortillas into my hand, said in a whisper: " now, when you buy the cheese, you'll have something to eat with it." With a cheese for two reals, my sworn friend and I made a hearty supper. He did for me many kind little offices, with a sort of meek fidelity, that touched me exceedingly. After our meal was finished, he went into the woods and brought me a calabash of water, standing uncovered while I drank it. I lay upon the ground, but all the fleas in the village, who had been without sustenance for two days, pounced in upon me in swarms. Added to this, every exposed part of the body was attacked by legions of musquitos, so that, with such enemies without and within, I never passed a more terrible night

CHAPTER XI.

THE ASCENT TO THE TABLE-LAND.

I was lying upon my back, with my handkerchief over my face, trying to imagine that I was asleep, when the welcome voice of the arriero shouted in my ear: "Ho! *Placero!* up and saddle!—the morning is coming and we must reach Tepic to-day." We fed our horses and sat on the ground for an hour before the first streak of dawn appeared. Three or four leagues of travel through a rich meadow-land brought us to the foot of the first ascent to the table-land. Our horses were fast failing, and we got off to walk up the stony trail. "I think we had better keep very close together," said my friend; "these woods are full of robbers, and they may attack us." Our path was fenced in by thorny thickets and tall clumps of cactus, and at every winding we were careful to have our arms in readiness. We climbed the first long ascent to a narrow plain, or shelf, from which we ascended again, finding always higher ridges above us. From the Abrevadero, a sort of inn or hospice standing alone in the woods, the hot, low country we left was visible nearly as far as Acaponeta; to one going towards Mazatlan, its dark-blue level might easily be mistaken for the sea. The Silla de San Juan was now to the west of us, and stood nearly five thousand feet in height. From the top of every successive ridge we overlooked a great extent of country, broken and cloven in all downward directions by the agency of some pre-Adamite flood, yet inclosing in many sheltered valleys and basins spots of singular fertility and beauty, which are watered through whole year from the cisterns of the mountains. It was truly, as the old lady at El Rosario said, "*un pais precioso.*"

We reached at noon a village called El Ingenio, about twelve leagues from Tepic. It lies in a warm valley planted with bananas and sugar-cane; the mountain streams are made to turn a number of mills, from which the place probably derives its name. Here the road from San Blas runs up through a narrow gorge and joins that from Mazatlan. We walked behind our horses all the afternoon, but as mine held out best, I gradually got ahead of the arriero. I halted several times for him to come up, but as he did not appear, I thought it advisable to push on to a good place of rest. My caminador had touched the bottom of his capability, and another day would have broken him down completely. Nevertheless, he had served me faithfully and performed miracles, considering his wasted condition. I drove him forward up ravines, buried in foliage and fragrant with blossoms; the golden globes of the oranges spangled the "embalméd darkness," as twilight settled on the mountains. Two leagues from Tepic, I reached the hacienda of La Meca, and quartered myself for the night. One of the rancheros wished to purchase my horse, and after some chaffering, I agreed to deliver him in Tepic for four dollars! The owner of the hacienda, on learning this, was greatly disappointed that I had not bargained with him, and urged me very strongly to break my word and sell him the horse for three dollars and a half! I told him I would not sell the animal for

5*

eight dollars, after having made a bargain ; he was enraged at this, but, as I could plainly see, respected me the more for it.

The young rancheros belonging to the hacienda amused themselves very much at my expense. A demon of fun seemed to possess them, and the simple sentences in my Spanish phrase-book excited them to yells of laughter. They were particularly curious to know my tastes and preferences, and on learning that I had never drank *mescal*, invited me to go with them and try it. We went down the road to a little hut, where a shelf with a bottle and two glasses upon it swinging under the thatched portico, signified "Liquor for Sale," to the passing arrieros. We entered and sat down among the family, who were at their scanty supper of rice and tortillas. The poor people offered me their own plates with a most genuine unsophisticated hospitality ; the rancheros told them whence I came, and they seemed anxious to learn something about my country. I tasted the *mescal*, which is stronger than brandy, and has a pungent oily flavor ; I should think its effects most pernicious if habitually drank. The people were curious to know about our Free School System of which they had heard by some means. None of them knew how to read, and they lamented most bitterly that education in Mexico was so difficult for their class. I was deeply touched by the exclamation of an old man, whose eyes trembled with tears as he spoke : " Ah, how beautiful a thing it is to be able to read of God !" then adding, in a softened tone, as if speaking to himself : " but I cannot read—I cannot read." I found many such persons among those ignorant rancheros—men who were conscious of their inferiority and desired most earnestly to be enlightened and improved.

Tepic is built on the first plateau of the table-land, and about half-way between the Silla de San Juan and an extinct volcano called San Guénguéy, which lifts its blackened brow high into the eastern sky. The plain, about fifteen miles in breadth, is for the most part moist meadow-land, threaded by several small streams. The city is girdled by pleasant gardens which hide everything from view on approaching, except the towers and dome of its cathedral. It is a solid well-built town of massive adobe houses mostly of one story, and divided by streets running at right angles. The general aspect of the place is dull and monotonous, with the exception of the plaza, which is one of the most beautiful in Mexico. A row of giant plane-trees runs around the four sides, shading the arched corridors of stone in which the traders display their fruits, trinkets, and articles of dress. There is an old stone fountain in the centre, around which, under canopies of grass-matting, are heaped piles of yellow bananas, creamy chirimoyas, oranges, and the scarlet, egg-like fruit of the Chinese pomegranate. All the gayety of the city seems to concentrate in the plaza, and, indeed, there is nothing else worth the traveler's notice, unless he is interested in manufactures—in which case he should visit the large cotton mills of Barron and Forbes in the vicinity. It is mainly through these mills that Tepic is known in the United States.

I had been directed to call at the posada of Doña Petra, but no one seemed to know the lady. Wandering about at random in the streets, I asked a boy to conduct me to some méson. As I rode along, following him, a group of tailors sitting at a street-corner, sewing, called out : " Americano !" " *No tiene ustéd cuidado*," said the boy, " *son mal criados*" (Don't mind them ; they have bad manners.) I followed him into the court-yard of a large building, where I was received by the *patron*, who gave my done-over horse to the charge of the mozo, telling me I was just in time for breakfast. My name was suddenly called from the opposite corridor; I turned about in surprise, and recognised the face of Mr. Jones of Guadalajara, whom I had met in Mazatlan. He had likewise just arrived, and was deep in the midst of a tempting salad and omelette, where I soon joined him. I had been in the house but a few minutes, when a heavy shower began, and continued several hours without cessation; it was the first of the *cabañuelos*, a week of rainy weather, which comes in the middle of the dry season. The purchaser of my horse did not make his appearance, notwithstanding I was ready to fulfil my part of the bargain. As soon as the rain was over, I went the round of the different mésons, to procure another horse, and at last made choice of a little brown mustang that paced admirably, giving my caminador and twenty dollars for him. I made arrangements to leave Tepic the next morning, for the journey from Mazatlan had cost me eight days, and nine hundred miles still lay between me and Vera Cruz, where I was obliged to be on the 16th of February.

Leaving the méson on a bright Sunday noon, I left the city by the Guadalajara road. The plaza was full of people, all in spotless holiday dress; a part of the exercises were performed in the portals of the cathedral, thus turning the whole square into a place of worship. At the tingle of the bell, ten thousand persons dropped on their knees, repeating their *aves* with a light, murmuring sound, that chimed pleasantly with the bubbling of the fountain. I stopped my horse and took off my sombrero till the prayer was over. The scenery beyond Tepic is very picturesque; the road crosses the plateau on which the city is built, and rounds the foot of San Guënguëy, whose summit, riven into deep gulfs between its pinnacles of rock, was half-hidden in clouds as I passed. I came

into a pretty valley, surrounded on all sides by rugged hills ; fields
of cane and rice dotted its surface, but the soil was much less fertile than in the rich bottoms of the Tierra Caliente.

My *priéto*—the Mexican term for a dark-brown horse—paced
finely, and carried me to the village of San Lionel, ten leagues
from Tepic, two hours before nightfall. I placed him securely in
the corral, deposited my saddle in an empty room, the key of which,
weighing about four pounds, was given into my possession for the
time being, and entered the kitchen. I found the entire household in a state of pleased anticipation ; a little girl, with wings of
red and white gauze, and hair very tightly twisted into ropy ring-
lets, sat on a chair near the door. In the middle of the little
plaza, three rancheros, with scarfs of crimson and white silk suspended from their shoulders and immense tinsel crowns upon their
heads, sat motionless on their horses, whose manes and tails were
studded with rosettes of different colored paper and streamers of
ribbons. These were, as I soon saw, part of the preparations for
a sacred dramatic spectacle—a representation, sanctioned by the
religious teachers of the people.

Against the wing-wall of the Hacienda del Mayo, which occupied one end of the plaza, was raised a platform, on which stood a
table covered with scarlet cloth. A rude bower of cane-leaves, on
one end of the platform, represented the manger of Bethlehem ;
while a cord, stretched from its top across the plaza to a hole in
the front of the church, bore a large tinsel star, suspended by a
hole in its centre. There was quite a crowd in the plaza, and
very soon a procession appeared, coming up from the lower part
of the village. The three kings took the lead ; the Virgin,
mounted on an ass that gloried in a gilded saddle and rose-be-
sprinkled mane and tail, followed them, led by the angel ; and

several women, with curious masks of paper, brought up the rear.
Two characters of the harlequin sort—one with a dog's head on
his shoulders and the other a bald-headed friar, with a huge hat
hanging on his back—played all sorts of antics for the diversion
of the crowd.   After making the circuit of the plaza, the Virgin
was taken to the platform, and entered the manger.   King Herod
took his seat at the scarlet table, with an attendant in blue coat
and red sash, whom I took to be his Prime Minister.   The three
kings remained on their horses in front of the church; but between
them and the platform, under the string on which the star was to
slide, walked two men in long white robes and blue hoods, with
parchment folios in their hands.   These were the Wise Men of
the East, as one might readily know from their solemn air, and
the mysterious glances which they cast towards all quarters of the
heavens.

In a little while, a company of women on the platform, concealed behind a curtain, sang an angelic chorus to the tune of " O
pescator dell'onda."   At the proper moment, the Magi turned
towards the platform, followed by the star, to which a string was conveniently attached, that it might be slid along the line.   The three
kings followed the star till it reached the manger, when they dismounted, and inquired for the sovereign whom it had led them to
visit.   They were invited upon the platform and introduced to
Herod, as the only king; this did not seem to satisfy them, and,
after some conversation, they retired.   By this time the star had
receded to the other end of the line, and commenced moving forward again, they following.   The angel called them into the manger, where, upon their knees, they were shown a small wooden
box, supposed to contain the sacred infant; they then retired,
and the star brought them back no more.   After this departure,

King Herod declared himself greatly confused by what he had witnessed, and was very much afraid this newly-found king would weaken his power. Upon consultation with his Prime Minister, the Massacre of the Innocents was decided upon, as the only means of security.

The angel, on hearing this, gave warning to the Virgin, who quickly got down from the platform, mounted her bespangled donkey and hurried off. Herod's Prime Minister directed all the children to be handed up for execution. A boy, in a ragged sarape, was caught and thrust forward; the Minister took him by the heels in spite of his kicking, and held his head on the table. The little brother and sister of the boy, thinking he was really to be decapitated, yelled at the top of their voices, in an agony of terror, which threw the crowd into a roar of laughter. King Herod brought down his sword with a whack on the table, and the Prime Minister, dipping his brush into a pot of white paint which stood before him, made a flaring cross on the boy's face. Several other boys were caught and served likewise; and, finally, the two harlequins, whose kicks and struggles nearly shook down the platform. The procession then went off up the hill, followed by the whole population of the village. All the evening there were fandangos in the méson, bonfires and rockets on the plaza, ringing of bells, and high mass in the church, with the accompaniment of two guitars, tinkling to lively polkas.

I left San Lionel early in the morning. The road, leaving the valley, entered the defiles of the mountains, crossing many a wild and rocky *barranca*. (A barranca nearly answers to the idea of our word "gulley," but is on a deeper and grander scale.) A beautiful species of pine already appeared, but in the warm hollows small plantations of bananas still flourished. I lost sight of San

Guënguëy, and after two hours of rough travel, came out on a mountain slope overlooking one of the most striking landscapes I ever beheld. In front, across a reach of high table-land, two lofty volcanic peaks rose far above the rim of the barren hills. To the left, away towards the east, extended a broad and lovely valley, dotted with villages and the green shimmer of fields, and hemmed in on all sides by mountains that touched the clouds. These lofty ranges—some of which were covered with trees to the summit, and some bleak and stony, despite their aerial hue of purple— make no abrupt transition from the bed of the valley : on the contrary, the latter seems to be formed by the gradual flattening of their bases. The whole scene wore a distinct, vaporless, amethyst tint, and the volcano of Zurubuco, though several leagues distant, showed every jag in the cold and silent lips of its crater.

I rode thirty miles, to the village of Santa Ysabel, before break-fasting, and still had twenty-one miles to Ahuacatlan, my stopping-place for the night. My road led down the beautiful valley, between fields of the *agave americana*. Sunset came on as I reached the foot of Zurubuco, and struck on a rocky path across a projecting spur. Here a most wonderful region opened before me. The pleasant valley disappeared, with everything that reminded me of life, and I was surrounded, as far as the vision extended, with the black waves of a lava sea. It was terrible as the gates of Tartarus—a wild, inexorable place, with no gleam of light on its chaotic features. The road was hewn with difficulty through the surgy crests of rock, which had stiffened to adamant, while tossing in their most tempestuous rage. The only thing like vegetation, was a tree with a red and bloated trunk, the bark of which peeled off in shreds,—apparently a sort of vegetable elephan-tiasis, as disgusting as the human specimens I saw on the Isthmus.

I passed this region with a sensation bordering on fear, welcoming the dusky twilight of the shaded road beyond, and the bright moon under whose rays I entered Ahuacatlan.

At the méson I found no one but the hostess and her two little sons; but the latter attended to my wants with a childish courtesy, and gravity withal, which were charming. The little fellows gave me the key to a room, saw my *priéto* properly cared for, and then sat down to entertain me till the tortillas were made and the eggs fried. They talked with much naïveté and a wisdom beyond their years. After supper they escorted me to my room, and took leave of me with: "*pasa usté muy buena noche!*" I arose in the cloudless dawn, rode through the gay, spacious plaza of the village, crossed another barranca, and reached Iztlan in time for breakfast. This is a beautiful place, embosomed in gardens, from the midst of which the church lifts its white tower. Beyond Iztlan, a delicious valley-picture lay before me. The dark red mountains, bristling with rock, formed nearly an even circle, inclosing a bowl about ten miles in diameter. Further down their sides, the plantations of the agave, or aloe, made a belt of silvery gray, and deep in the fertile bosom of the plain, the gardens and orange groves, with sparkling glimpses of streams between the black loam, freshly ploughed, and the fields of young cane, of a pale golden green, basked in the full light of the sun. Far off, over the porphyry rim of the basin, a serrated volcanic peak stood up against the stainless blue of the sky. It was one of those rare chances in nature, when scenery, color, climate, and the sentiment of the spot, are in entire and exquisite harmony.

Leaving this valley, which was like a crystal or a piece of perfect enamel, buried in a region that Nature had left in the rough, I climbed a barren hill, which terminated at the brink of

the grand Barranca—a tremendous chasm, dividing two sections
of the table-land. Two thousand feet below, at the level of the
Tierra Caliente, lay a strip of Eden-like richness and beauty, but
the mountains which walled it on both sides were dark, sterile and
savage. Those opposite to me rose as far above the level of the
ledge on which I stood, as their bases sank below it. Their appearance was indescribably grand ; for the most perfect and sublime effect of a mountain is to be had neither from base nor
summit, but a station midway between the two and separated from
it. The road descending to Plan de Barranca, a little village at
the bottom of the chasm, is built with great labor along the very
verge of giddy precipices, or notched under the eaves of crags which
threaten to topple down upon it. The ascent of the opposite
steep is effected by a stony trail, barely large enough for two
mules to pass, up the side of a wide crevice in the mountain-wall.
Finally, the path appears to fail ; the precipice falls sheer on one
side ; the bare crag rises on the other. But a sudden twist
around the corner of a rock reveals a narrow cleft, terminating in
the lower shelf of the table-land above. Looking back after I
had scaled this, an *atajo* of mules which followed me, appeared
to be emerging from the bowels of the earth. The road crossing
the barranca is nearly fifteen miles in length. Large numbers of
workmen are engaged in completing it for vehicles, and over the
deepest chasm a bridge is being constructed by the State of Jalisco.
Five years, however, is the shortest period named for the completion of the work, up to which time the barranca will remain
impassable except for mules. The line of stages to Tepic, which
is greatly demanded by the increase of travel, cannot therefore be
perfected before that time ; but Señor Zurutuza, the proprietor of
the diligence lines, proposes opening a communication immediately,

by means of a mule-post across the barranca. From Tepic to San Blas is but a day's journey, so that the chain of comfortable travel will then reach nearly from ocean to ocean.

My *priéto* began to feel the effects of the hard hills and thin air of the upper region, and I therefore stopped for the night at the inn of Mochitilte, an immense building, sitting alone like a fortress among the hills. The key of a large, cheerless room, daubed with attempts at fresco ornament, was given to me, and a supper served up in a cold and gloomy hall. The wind blew chill from the heights on either side, and I found *priéto's* blanket a welcome addition to my own, in the matter of bedding.

CHAPTER XII.

I SLEPT soundly in my frescoed chamber, fed *priéto*, and was off by sunrise. The road ascended the valley for several leagues, to the rim of the table-land, with high, barren mountains on either hand. Before crossing its edge I turned to look down into the basin I had left. A few streaks of dusky green varied its earthen hue; far off, in its very bottom, the front of the méson of Mochitilte shone like a white speck in the sunrise, and the blue walls of the barranca filled up the farthest perspective. I now entered on a broad, barren plain, bordered by stony mountains and holding in its deepest part a shallow lake, which appeared to be fast drying in the sun. The scenery strikingly resembled that of some parts of California, towards the end of the rainy season.

The little town of Magdalena, where I breakfasted, sits beside the lake, at the foot of a glen through which the road again enters the hills. The waters of a clear stream trickle down through its streets and keep green the gardens of splendid orange-trees which gleam behind the gray adobe walls. At the méson I gave priéto a sheaf of *oja* and two hours' rest before starting for the town of Tequila. "*No quiere ustè tomar ausilio ?—hay muchos ladrones en el camino ;*" (Don't you want a guard ?—the road is full of robbers,) asked the vaquero of the house. " Every traveler," he continued, " takes a guard as far as Tequila, for which he pays each man a dollar." I told him I had no particular fear of the robbers, and would try it alone. " You are very courageous," he remarked, " but you will certainly be attacked unless you take me as an *ausilio*."

Soon after leaving the town I met a *conducta* of a hundred soldiers, escorting about fifty specie-laden mules. The officers were finely mounted, but the men, most of whom had broad, swarthy Indian faces, trudged along in the dust. Some of them greeted me with : " *Como va, paisano ?*" some with " How do you do ?" and others with a round English oath, but all imagining, apparently, that they had made the same salutation. As I was passing, a tawny individual, riding with one of the officers, turned about and addressed me in English. He was an American, who had been several years in the country, and was now on his way to California, concerning which he wanted some information. Notwithstanding he was bound to San Blas and had all his funds packed on one of the mules, he seemed still undecided whether to embark for San Francisco, and like most of the other emigrants I met, insisted strongly on my opinion as to the likelihood of *his* success. The road now entered a narrow pass, following the dry bed of a stream, whose channel was worn about twenty feet deep in the earth. Its many abrupt twists and windings afforded unequalled chances for the guerillas, especially as the pass was nearly three leagues in length, without a single habitation on the road. My friend, Lieutenant Beale, was chased by a party of robbers, in this very place, on his express journey across Mexico, in the summer of 1848. I did not meet with a single soul, although it was not later than the middle of the afternoon. The recent passing of the *conducta* had probably frightened the robbers away from the vicinity.

After riding two hours in the hot afternoon sun, which shone down into the pass, a sudden turn disclosed to me a startling change of scenery. From the depths of the scorched hills, I came at once upon the edge of a bluff, several hundred feet high, down which the road wound in a steep and tortuous descent. Below and before me extended a plain of twenty miles in length, entirely covered with fields of the *maguey*. At my very feet lay the city of Tequila, so near that it seemed a stone might be thrown upon the square towers of its cathedral. The streets, the gardens, the housetops and the motley groups of the populace, were as completely unveiled to my observation as if Asmodeus had been my traveling companion. Around the plain, which now lay basking in the mellow light of the low sun, ran a circle of mural mountains, which, high and blue as they were, sank into nothing before the stupendous bulk of a black volcanic peak rising behind Tequila. The whole scene, with its warm empurpled hues, might have served, if not for the first circle of Dante's Paradise, at least for that part of Purgatory which lay next to it.

I rode down into the city, crossing several arroyos, which the floods gathered by the volcano had cut deeper into the plain. At the *Mèson de San Josè*—the only inn in the place—I found a large company of soldiers quartered for the night. The inner *patio* or courtyard, with its stables, well, and massive trough of hewn stone, was appropriated to their horses, and groups of swarthy privates, in dusty blue uniforms, filled the corridors. I obtained a dark room for myself, and a corner of one of the stalls for *priéto*, where I was obliged to watch until he had finished his corn, and keep off his military aggressors. The women were all absent, and I procured a few tortillas and a cup of pepper-sauce, with some difficulty. The place looked bleak and cheerless after dark, and for this reason, rather than its cut-throat reputation, I made but a single stroll to the plaza, where a number of rancheros sat beside their piles of fruit and grain, in the light of smoky torches, hoisted on poles. The méson was full of fleas, who seemed to relish my blood better than that of the soldiers, for I believe they all paid me a visit in the course of the night.

When I arose, the sun, just above the hills, was shining down the long street that led to Guadalajara. I had a journey of eighteen leagues to make, and it was time to be on the road; so, without feeding my horse, I saddled and rode away. A little more than four leagues across the plain, brought me to the town of Amatitlan; where, at a miserable mud building, dignified by the name of a méson, I ordered breakfast, and a *mano de oja* for my horse. There was none in the house, but one of the neighbors began shelling a quantity of the ripe ears. When I came to pay, I gave her a Mexican dollar, which she soon brought back, saying that it had been pronounced counterfeit at a *tienda*, or shop, across the way. I then gave her another, which she returned, with the same story, after which I gave her a third, saying she must change it, for I would give her no more. The affairs of a few hours later caused me to remember and understand the meaning of this little circumstance. At the *tienda*, a number of fellows in greasy sarapes were grouped, drinking mescal, which they offered me. I refused to join them : " *es la ultima vez*," (it is the last time,) said one of them, though what he meant, I did not then know.

It was about ten in the forenoon when I left Amatitlan. The road entered on a lonely range of hills, the pedestal of an abrupt spur standing out from the side of the volcano. The soil was covered with stunted shrubs and a growth of long yellow grass. I could see the way for half a league before and behind; there was no one in sight—not even a boy-arriero, with his two or three donkeys. I rode leisurely along, looking down into a deep ravine on my right and thinking to myself; "that is an excellent place for robbers to lie in wait; I think I had better load my pistol"— which I had fired off just before reaching Tequila. Scarcely had this thought passed through my mind, when a little bush beside the road seemed to rise up ; I turned suddenly, and, in a breath, the two barrels of a musket were before me, so near and surely aimed, that I could almost see the bullets at the bottom. The weapon was held by a ferocious-looking native, dressed in a pink calico shirt and white pantaloons ; on the other side of me stood a second, covering me with another double-barreled musket, and a little in the rear, appeared a third. I had walked like an unsuspecting mouse, into the very teeth of the trap laid for me.

"Down with your pistols !" cried the first, in a hurried whisper. So silently and suddenly had all this taken place, that I sat still a moment, hardly realizing my situation. "Down with your pistols and dismount !" was repeated, and this time the barrels came a little nearer my breast. Thus solicited, I threw down my single pistol—the more readily because it was harmless—and got off my horse. Having secured the pistol, the robbers went to the rear, never for a moment losing their aim. They then ordered me to lead my horse off the road, by a direction which they pointed out. We went down the side of the ravine for about a quarter of a mile to a patch of bushes and tall grass, out of view from the road, where they halted, one of them returning, apparently to keep watch. The others, deliberately levelling their pieces at me, commanded me to lie down on my face—"*la boca à tierra !*" I cannot say that I felt alarmed : it had always been a part of my belief that the shadow of Death falls before him—that the man doomed to die by violence feels the chill before the blow has been struck. As I never felt more positively alive than at that moment, I judged my time had not yet come. I pulled off my coat and vest, at their command, and threw them on the grass, saying : "Take what you want, but don't detain me long." The fellow in a pink calico shirt, who appeared to have some authority over the other two, picked up my coat, and, one after the other, turned all the pockets inside out. I felt a secret satisfaction at his blank look when he opened my purse and poured the few dollars it contained into a pouch he carried in his belt. "How is it," said he, "that you have no more money ?" "I don't own much," I answered, "but there is quite enough for you." I had, in fact, barely sufficient in coin for a ride to Mexico, the most of my funds having been invested in a draft on that city. I believe I did not lose more than twenty-five dollars by this attack. "At least," I said to the robbers, "you'll not take the papers"—among which was my draft. "*No*," he replied, "*no me valen nada.*" (They are worth nothing to me.)

Having searched my coat, he took a hunting-knife which I carried, (belonging, however, to Lieut. Beale,) examined the blade and point, placed his piece against a bush behind him and came up to me, saying, as he held the knife above my head : "Now put your hands behind you, and don't move, or I shall strike." The other then laid down his musket and advanced to bind me. They were evidently adepts in the art : all their movements were so carefully timed, that any resistance would have been against dangerous odds. I did not consider my loss sufficient to justify any desperate risk, and did as they commanded. With the end of my horse's lariat, they bound my wrists firmly together, and having me thus secure, sat down to finish their inspection more leisurely. My feelings during this proceeding were oddly hetero-geneous—at one moment burning with rage and shame at having neglected the proper means of defence, and the next, ready to burst into a laugh at the decided novelty of my situation. My blanket having been spread on the grass, everything was emptied into it. The robbers had an eye for the curious and incompre-hensible, as well as the useful. They spared all my letters, books and papers, but took my thermometer, compass and card-case, together with a number of drawing-pencils, some soap, (a thing the Mexicans never use,) and what few little articles of the toilette I carried with me. A bag hanging at my saddle-bow, con-taining ammunition, went at once, as well as a number of oranges and cigars in my pockets, the robbers leaving me *one* of the latter, as a sort of consolation for my loss.

Between Mazatlan and Tepic, I had carried a doubloon in the hollow of each foot, covered by the stocking. It was well they had been spent for *priéto*, for they would else have certainly been discovered. The villains unbuckled my spurs, jerked off my boots and examined the bottoms of my pantaloons, ungirthed the saddle and shook out the blankets, scratched the heavy guard of the bit to see whether it was silver, and then, apparently satisfied that they had made the most of me, tied everything together in a corner of my best blanket. "Now," said the leader, when this was done, "shall we take your horse?" This question was of course a mockery; but I thought I would try an experiment, and so answered in a very decided tone: "No; you shall not. I *must* have him; I am going to Guadalajara, and I cannot get there without him. Besides, he would not answer at all for your business." He made no reply, but took up his piece, which I noticed was a splendid article and in perfect order, walked a short distance towards the road, and made a signal to the third robber. Suddenly he came back, saying: " Perhaps you may get hungry before night—here is something to eat ;" and with that he placed one of my oranges and half a dozen tortillas on the grass beside me. " *Mil gracias*," said I, " but how am I to eat without hands ?" The other then coming up, he said, as they all three turned to leave me : " Now we are going ; we have more to carry than we had before we met you ; adios !" This was insulting— but there are instances under which an insult must be swallowed.

I waited till no more of them could be seen, and then turned to my horse, who stood quietly at the other end of the lariat : " Now, *priéto*," I asked, " how are we to get out of this scrape ?" He said nothing, but I fancied I could detect an inclination to laugh in the twitching of his nether lip. However, I went to work at extricating myself—a difficult matter, as the rope was tied in several knots. After tugging a long time, I made a twist which the India-rubber man might have envied, and to the great danger of my spine, succeeded in forcing my body through my arms. Then, loosening the knots with my teeth, in half an hour I was free again. As I rode off, I saw the three robbers at some distance, on the other side of the ravine.

It is astonishing how light one feels after being robbed. A sensation of complete independence came over me ; my horse, even, seemed to move more briskly, after being relieved of my blankets. I tried to comfort myself with the thought that this was a genuine adventure, worth one experience—that, perhaps, it was better to lose a few dollars than have even a robber's blood on my head ; but it would not do. The sense of the outrage and

indignity was strongest, and my single desire was the unchristian
one of revenge. It is easy to philosophize on imaginary premises,
but actual experience is the best test of human nature. Once, it
had been difficult for me to imagine the feeling that would prompt
a man to take the life of another ; now, it was clear enough. In
spite of the threats of the robbers, I looked in their faces sufficiently to know them again, in whatever part of the world I might
meet them. I recognized the leader—a thick-set, athletic man,
with a short, black beard—as one of the persons I had seen
lounging about the *tienda*, in Amatitlan, which explained the
artifice that led me to display more money than was prudent. It
was evidently a preconceived plan to plunder me at all hazards,
since, coming from the Pacific, I might be supposed to carry a
booty worth fighting for.

I rode on rapidly, over broad, barren hills, covered with patches
of chapparal, and gashed with deep arroyos. These are the usual
hiding-places of the robbers, and I kept a sharp look-out, inspect-
ing every rock and clump of cactus with a peculiar interest.
About three miles from the place of my encounter, I passed a
spot where there had been a desperate assault eighteen months
previous. The robbers came upon a camp of soldiers and traders
in the night, and a fight ensued, in which eleven of the latter were
killed. They lie buried by the road-side, with a few black crosses
to mark the spot, while directly above them stands a rough
gibbet, on which three of the robbers, who were afterwards taken,
swing in chains. I confess to a decided feeling of satisfaction,
when I saw that three, at least, had obtained their deserts.
Their long black hair hung over their faces, their clothes
were dropping in tatters, and their skeleton-bones protruded
through the dry and shrunken flesh. The thin, pure air of the

table-land had prevented decomposition, and the vultures and buzzards had been kept off by the nearness of the bodies to the road. It is said, however, that neither wolves nor vultures will touch a dead Mexican, his flesh being always too highly seasoned by the red-pepper he has eaten. A large sign was fastened above this ghastly spectacle, with the words, in large letters: "ASI CASTIGA LA LEY EL LADRON Y EL ASESINO." (Thus the law punishes the robber and the assassin.)

Towards the middle of the afternoon, I reached a military station called La Venta, seven leagues from Guadalajara. Thirty or forty idle soldiers were laughing and playing games in the shade. I rode up to the house and informed the officer of my loss, mentioning several circumstances by which the robbers might be identified; but the zealous functionary merely shrugged his shoulders and said nothing. A proper distribution of half the soldiers who lay idle in this guard-house, would have sufficed to make the road perfectly secure. I passed on, with a feeling of indignation against the country and its laws, and hurried my priéto, now nearly exhausted, over the dusty plain. I had ascended beyond the tropical heats, and, as night drew on, the temperature was fresh almost to chilliness. The robbers had taken my cravat and vest, and the cold wind of the mountains, blowing upon my bare neck gave me a violent nervous pain and toothache, which was worse than the loss of my money. Priéto panted and halted with fatigue, for he had already traveled fifty miles; but I was obliged to reach Guadalajara, and by plying a stick in lieu of the abstracted spur, kept him to his pace. At dusk I passed through Sapopa, a small village, containing a splendid monastery, belonging to the monks of the order of Guadalupe. Beyond it, I overtook, in the moonlight, the family of a ranchero, jogging along on their mules and repeating paternosters, whether for protection against robbers or cholera, I could not tell. The plain was crossed by deep, water-worn arroyos, over which the road was bridged. An hour and a half of this bleak, ghostly travel brought me to the suburbs of Guadalajara—greatly to the relief of *priéto*, for he began to stagger, and I believe could not have carried me a mile further.

I was riding at random among the dark adobe houses, when an old padre, in black cassock and immense shovel-hat, accosted me. "*Estrangero?*" he inquired; "*Si, padre*," said I. "But," he continued, "do you know that it is very dangerous to be here alone?" Several persons who were passing, stopped near us, out of curiosity. "Begone!" said he, "what business have you to stop and listen to us?"—then, dropping his voice to a whisper, he added: "Guadalajara is full of robbers; you must be careful how you wander about after night; do you know where to go?" I answered in the negative. "Then," said he, "go to the Méson de la Mercéd; they are honest people there, and you will be perfectly safe; come with me and I'll show you the way." I followed him for some distance, till we were near the place, when he put me in the care of "Ave Maria Santissima," and left. I found the house without difficulty, and rode into the court-yard. The people, who seemed truly honest, sympathized sincerely for my mishap, and thought it a great marvel that my life had been spared For myself, when I lay down on the tiled floor to pass another night of sleepless martyrdom to fleas and the toothache, I involuntarily said, with a slight variation of Touchstone's sage reflection: "Aye, now I am in Guadalajara; the more fool I; when I was at home I was in a better place; but travelers must be content."

CHAPTER XIII.

THREE DAYS IN GUADALAJARA.

When I got off my horse at the Méson de la Mercéd, I told the host and the keeper of the *fonda* that I had been robbed, that I had no money, and did not expect to have any for two or three days. "*No hace nada,*" said they, "you may stay as long as you like." So they gave my horse a sheaf of *oja* and myself a supper of tortillas and pepper-sauce. The old lady who kept the fonda was of half-Castilian blood, and possessed all the courtesy of her white ancestors, with the quickness and vivacity of the Indian. She was never tired of talking to me about the strangers who had stopped at the méson,—especially of one whom she called Don Julio, who, knowing little Spanish, frequently accosted her as "mule!" or "donkey!" for want of some other word. She would mimic him with great apparent delight. She had three daughters—Felipa, Mariquita and Concepcion—of whom the two former were very beautiful. They were employed in the manufacture of rebosas, and being quite skilful in tending the machines, earned a dollar a day—a considerable sum for Mexico. Concepcion was married, and had a son named Zenobio—a very handsome, sprightly little fellow, with dark, humid, lustrous eyes. The circumstance of my remembering and calling each one by name, seemed to please them highly, and always at meal-time they gathered around the table, asking me innumerable questions about my country and my travels.

My first move next morning was to find the Diligence Office. I went into the main plaza, which is a beautiful square, shaded by orange trees, and flanked on two sides by the picturesque front of the Cathedral and the Government Palace. As I was passing the latter building, one of the sentinels hailed me. Supposing it to be meant in derision, I paid no attention to it, but presently a sergeant, accompanied by two men, came after me. One of the latter accosted me in English, saying that it was so long since he had seen an American, he hoped I would stop and talk with him He was a Scotchman, who for some reason had enlisted for a year and had already served about half of his time. He complained bitterly of the bad treatment of the men, who, according to his story, were frequently on the point of starvation. The Mexican soldiers are not furnished with rations, but paid a small sum daily, on which they support themselves. As the supplies from head-quarters are very irregular, and a system of appropriation is practised by all the officers through whose hands they must come, the men are sometimes without food for a day or two, and never receive more than is barely sufficient for their wants. The poor Scotchman was heartily sick of his situation and told me he would have deserted long before, only that he had no other clothes in which to disguise himself.

At the office of the Diligence, I found the *administrador*, Don Lorenzo del Castaño, to whom I related my story and showed my draft. "*Es superior*," said he, after examining it, and then told me to call the next morning, as he would see a merchant in the meantime, who, he was sure, would pay me the amount. Drafts on the city of Mexico were at a premium of two per cent. and he had no difficulty in getting it accepted. The money, however, was paid to me in quarter-dollars, reals and medios, which it took me more than an hour to count. I went back to the office, with a heavy canvas-bag in each pocket, paid all the money to the administrador, who gave me a ticket for the next stage to Mexico, and an order for the residue on all the agents of the line. By exhibiting these orders at the different stopping-places on the road, the traveler receives credit for all his expenses, the amount at each place being endorsed at the bottom, and the remainder, if any, paid on his arrival at Mexico. By this means, he is saved the necessity of taking any money with him, and may verify the old Latin proverb by whistling in the face of the robber. I was thus led, perforce, to give up my original plan of traveling on horseback to Mexico, by way of Lake Chapala, Zamora, the ancient city of Morelia and the valley of Toluca. This route offered less of general interest than that of Lagos and Guanajuato, but had the attraction of being little traveled by strangers and little known. Perhaps I lost nothing by the change, for the hills near Zamora are robber-ground, and I had no desire to look into the barrels of three or four leveled muskets a second time.

I found Guadalajara in a state of terror and prayers. For a month previous the inhabitants had been expecting the arrival of the Cholera, now that its ravages in Durango and Zacatecas were over. The city authorities were doing everything in their power to hasten its approach, by prohibiting all public amusements and instituting solemn religious festivals. The Cathedral was at all times crowded with worshippers, the Host frequently carried through the streets, gunpowder burned and rockets sent up to propitiate the Virgin. As yet no case had been reported in the

6*

city, though there were rumors of several in the neighboring villages. The convicts were brought out every morning in long gangs, chained together, each man carrying a broom made of small twigs. Commencing with the centre of the city, they were kept sweeping the whole day, till all the principal streets were left without a particle of dust or filth. The clanking of their fetters was constantly heard in some part of the city; the officers who walked behind them carried short whips, with which they occasionally went up and down the lines, giving each man a blow. This daily degradation and abuse of criminals was cruel and repulsive. The men, low and debased as they were, could not have been entirely devoid of shame, the existence of which always renders reclamation possible; but familiarity with ignominy soon breeds a hardened indifference which meets the pride of honesty with an equal pride of evil.

Guadalajara is considered the most beautiful city in Mexico. Seated on a shelf of the table-land, between three and four thousand feet above the sea, it enjoys a milder climate than the capital, and while its buildings lack very little of the magnificence of the latter, its streets are a model of cleanliness and order. The block fronting on the north side of the plaza, is a single solid edifice of stone, called the *Cortal*, with a broad corridor, supported on stone arches, running around it. The adjoining block is built on the same plan, and occupied entirely by shops of all kinds. Shielded alike from rain and sun, it is a favorite promenade, and always wears a gay and busy aspect. The intervals between the pillars, next the street, are filled with cases of toys, pictures, gilt images of saints, or gaudy slippers, sarapes and rebosas. Here the rancheros may be seen in abundance, buying ornaments for the next festivals. Venders of fruit sit at the corners, their mats filled with fragrant and gleaming pyramids, and the long shelves of cool barley-water and *tepache*, ranged in glasses of alternate white and purple, attract the thirsty idler. Here and there a group is gathered around a placard pasted on the wall—some religious edict of the cholera-fearing authorities, a list of the fortunate tickets in the last lottery, or the advertisement of a magnificent cock-fight that is to come off in the old town of Uruàpan. The bulletin at the lottery-office is always surrounded; rancheros, housemaids, padres and robbers come up, pull out their tickets from under their cassocks and dirty sarapes, compare the numbers and walk away with the most complete indifference at their ill luck. The shops belonging to different trades are always open; tailors and shoemakers frequently sit in groups in the open corridor, with their work on their knees, undisturbed by the crowds that pass to and fro. I spent several hours daily in the *cortal*, never tiring of the picturesque life it exhibited.

It is remarkable how soon a man's misfortunes are made public. The second day of my stay in Guadalajara, I believe I was known to most of the inhabitants as " the American who was robbed." This, together with my rugged and dusty suit of clothing, (what was left of it,) made me the subject of general notice; so, after selling my draft, I hastened to disguise myself in a white shirt and a pair of Mexican pantaloons. One benefit of this notoriety was, that it was the means of my becoming acquainted with two or three American residents, and through them, with several intelligent and agreeable citizens. I never entered a place under such woful auspices, nor passed the time of my stay more delightfully. In walking about the streets I was often hailed with the word " *wistli !*" by some of the lower class. From the sound I thought it might possibly be an old Aztec word of salutation; but one day I met a man, who, as he said it, held up a bottle of mescal, and I saw at once that he meant *whiskey*. The fact that it was constantly repeated to me as an American, gave rather a curious inference as to the habits of the emigrants who had passed through the city before me.

The appearance of Guadalajara on Sunday morning was very cheerful and beautiful. Everybody was in the streets, though not more than half the shops were closed ; the bells rang at intervals from the cathedral and different churches; the rancheros flocked in from the country, the men in snow-white shirts and blue calzoneros, the women in their best rebosas and petticoats of some gay color ; and the city, clean swept by the convicts, and flooded with warm sunshine, seemed to give itself up truly to a holiday. I walked down along the banks of the little river which divides it into two unequal parts. The pink towers of the Bishop's Palace rose lightly in the air ; up a long street, the gateway of the Convent of San Francisco stood relieved against a shaded court-yard ; the palms in some of the near gardens rustled in a slow breeze, but the dark shafts of the cypress were silent and immovable. Along the parapets of the bridges, the rancheros displayed their faggots of sugar-cane and bunches of bananas, chatting gaily with each other, and with their neighbors who passed by on mules or asses. I visited most of the churches during the time of service. Many of them are spacious and might be made impressive, but they are all disfigured by a tawdry and tasteless style of ornament, a profusion of glaring paint and gilding, ghastly statues, and shocking pictures. The church of the Convent of San Francisco is partly an exception to this censure ; in a sort of loggia it has a large painting of the Last Supper, by a Mexican artist, which is truly a work of great beauty. In the body of the church are several undoubted originals by Murillo, though not of his best period; I did not see them. The cathedral, more majestic in proportion, is likewise more simple and severe in its details; its double row of columns, forming three aisles, the central one supporting a low dome, have a grand effect when viewed from the entrance. It was constantly filled with worshippers, most of whom were driven thither by the approach of the cholera. Even in passing its door, as they crossed the plaza, the inhabitants uncovered or made the sign of the cross—an extent of devotion which I never witnessed out of Mexico.

I found great source for amusement in the carriages collected near the doors during mass-hour. They were all the manufacture of the country, and the most of them dated from the last century. The running works were of immense size, the four wheels sustaining a massive and elaborately carved frame, rising five or six feet from the ground, and about twelve feet in length. In the centre of this, suspended in some miraculous manner, hung a large wooden globe, with a door in each side—a veritable Noah's Ark in form and solidity, and capable of concealing a whole family (and the Mexican families are always large) in its hollow maw. These machines were frequently made still more ridiculous by the pair of dwarfed, starved mules, hitched to the tongue, so far in advance that they seemed to be running away from the mountain which pursued and was about to overwhelm them. I concluded, however, after some reflection, that they were peculiarly adapted to the country. In case of revolution they would be not only bullet but bomb proof, and as there are no good roads among the mountains, they would roll from top to bottom, or shoot off a precipice, without danger to the family within. There are several extensive carriage manufactories in Guadalajara, but the modern fabrics more nearly resemble those of our own cities, retaining only the heavy, carved frame-work, on which the body rests.

In the afternoon I went with some friends to make a *paseo* on the Alameda. This is a beautiful square on the border of the city, shaded with fine trees, and traversed by pleasant walks, radiating from fountains in the centre. It is surrounded by a hedge of roses, which bloom throughout the whole year, covering with a fragrant shade the long stone benches on which the citizens repose, Don and ranchero mingled together, smoking their puros and cigaritos. The drive is around the outside of the Alameda; I saw but a small part of the fashion of Guadalajara, as most of the families were remaining at home to invite the cholera. There were some handsome turn-outs, and quite a number of splendid horses, ridden in the Mexican style, which is perfection itself— horse and rider moving as one creature, and having, apparently, but one soul. The Mexican horses are all sprung from the Arabic and Andalusian stock introduced into the country by Cortez, and those large bands which run wild on the plains of San Joaquin and in the Camanche country, probably differ but slightly from the Arab horse of the present day.

A still more beautiful scene awaited us in the evening. The *paseo* is then transferred to the plaza, and all the fashionable population appears on foot—a custom which I found in no other Mexican city. I went there at nine o'clock. The full moon was shining down over the cathedral towers; the plaza was almost as distinct as by day, except that the shadows were deeper; the white arches and pillars of the *cortal* were defined brilliantly against the black gloom of the corridor, and the rows of orange trees, with their leaves glittering in the moonlight, gave out a rare and exquisite odor from their hidden blossoms. We sat down on one of the benches, so near the throng of promenaders passing around the plaza, that their dresses brushed our feet.   The ladies were in full dress, with their heads uncovered, and there were many specimens of tropic beauty among them.   The faint clear olive of their complexion, like a warm sunset-light on alabaster— the deep, dark, languishing eye, with the full drooping lid that would fain conceal its fire—the ripe voluptuous lip—the dark hair whose silky waves would have touched the ground had they been unbound—and the pliant grace and fullness of the form, formed together a type of beauty, which a little queenly ambition would have moulded into a living Cleopatra.   A German band in front of the cathedral played " God save the King" and some of the melodies of the Fatherland.   About ten o'clock, the throng began to disperse ; we sat nearly an hour longer, enjoying the delicious moonlight, coolness and fragrance, and when I lay down again on the tiles, so far from thinking of Touchstone, I felt glad and grateful for having seen Guadalajara.

Among the Guadalajarans I met was Don Ramon Luna, a gentleman of great intelligence and refinement.   His father emigrated from Spain as a soldier in the ranks, but by prudence, energy and native talent, succeeded in amassing a large fortune.   Don Ramon spoke English and French with great fluency, and was, moreover, very enthusiastic on the subject of Mexican antiquities. At his ranche, a few leagues from Guadalajara, he had, as he informed me, a large number of ancient idols and fossil remains, which the workmen had collected by his order.   I regretted that the shortness of my stay did not permit me to call on Padre Najar, of the Convent del Carmen, who formerly resided in Philadelphia, and published a very able work on the Otomai language.

The diligence was to start on Monday.   On Saturday afternoon

I sold my horse to a sort of trader living in the méson, for seven dollars, as he was somewhat worn out, and horses were cheap in Guadalajara. The parting with my good hosts the next day was rather more difficult, and I was obliged to make a positive promise of return within three years, before they would consent that I should go. After I had obtained some money and paid them for my board, the old lady told me that thenceforth she would only charge half-price for every meal I chose to take in her house. "Thanks to the Supreme King," said she, "I have not been so much in need that I should treat friends and strangers both alike." After this, I only paid a medio for my dinner of eggs, frijoles, lantecas and chili colorado.   On Sunday night I rolled up my few possessions in my sarape, took leave of the family and went to the *Casa de Diligencias* to spend the night.   The old hostess threw her arms around me and gave me a hearty embrace, and the three daughters followed her example.   I did not dislike this expression of friendship and regret, for they were quite beautiful. As I went down the court-yard, the voice of the mother followed me : "Go with Ave Maria Purisima, and do not forget Maria de la Ascencion Hidalgo !"

CHAPTER XIV.

THE mozo awoke me shortly after three o'clock, and before I had finished dressing, brought me a cup of foaming chocolate and a biscuit. The only other passenger was a student from Tepic, on his return to college, in Mexico. The stage already waited for us, and we had no sooner taken our seats on the leather cushions, than "*vamonos!*" cried the driver, the whip cracked and the wheels thundered along the silent, moonlit streets. The morning was chill, and there was little in the dim glimpses of adobe walls and blank fields on either hand, to interest us; so we lay back in the corners and took another nap.

The style of diligence travel in Mexico is preferable to that of any other country. The passenger is waked at three o'clock in the morning, has a cup of chocolate brought him, (and no one has drank chocolate who has not drank it there) takes his seat, and has nearly reached the end of the second post by sunrise. The heavy stage, of Troy manufacture, is drawn by six horses, four leaders abreast, who go at a dashing gallop as long as the road is level. About eleven o'clock a breakfast of six or eight courses is served up in good style, the coachman waiting until the last man has leisurely finished. There is no twanging of the horn and cry of

" All ready !" before one has bolted the first mouthful. Off again,
there is no stoppage till the day's journey is over, which is generally about four o'clock, allowing ample time for a long walk and
sight-seeing before dinner.

The second post brought us to the Rio Santiago, which I had
crossed once between Mazatlan and Tepic. We got out to look
at the old stone bridge and the mist of a cataract that rose above
the banks, two or three hundred yards below. Our road lay across
broad, stony tracts of country, diversified by patches of cactus;
in the distance, the mountain parapet of a still higher table-land
was to be seen. The third post, thirty miles from Guadalajara,
was at the village of Zapotlanejo, where the cholera had already
appeared. The groom who assisted in harnessing our fresh horses,
informed us that twenty persons had died of it. The place looked
quiet and half-deserted; many of the houses were studded with
little wooden crosses, stuck into the chinks of the adobes. The
village of Tepatitlan, which we passed during the forenoon, was
likewise a cholera locality. We dashed through it and over a bare,
bleak upland, many leagues in width, in the middle of which stood
the Rancho de la Tierra Colorada, (Ranche of the Red Earth) our
breakfast-place.

During the afternoon we crossed a very rough and stony barranca. The chasm at the bottom was spanned by a fine bridge,
and eight cream-colored mules were in readiness to take us up the
ascent. Even after reaching the level, the road was terribly rough,
and the bounds which our stage made as it whirled along, threatened to disjoint every limb in our bodies. I received a stunning
blow on the crown of my head, from being thrown up violently
against the roof. We were truly rejoiced when, late in the afternoon, we saw the little town of San Miguel before us, in a hollow

dip of the plain. We finished a ride of ninety miles as we drove into it, and found the stage from Lagos already before the hotel. The town did not boast a single " sight," so my companion and I took a siesta until dinner was announced.

The next morning our route lay over the dreary table-land, avoiding the many chasms and barrancas with which its surface was seamed : often running upon a narrow ridge, with a gaping hollow on each side. The rancheros were ploughing in some places, but the greater part of the soil seemed to be given up to pasturage. The fields were divided by walls of stone, but frequently, in the little villages, a species of cactus had been planted so as to form gardens and corrals, its straight, single pillars standing side by side, to the height of ten feet, with scarcely a crevice between. The people we met, were more hale and ruddy in their appearance than those of the Tierra Caliente. As they galloped alongside the stage, with their hats off, speaking with the driver, I thought I had never seen more lightly and strongly made forms, or more perfect teeth. When they laughed, their mouths seemed to blaze with the sparkling white rows exhibited. Towards noon, we saw, far ahead, the tops of two towers, that appeared to rise out of the earth. They belonged to the church of San Juan de Los Lagos, the place of the great Annual Fair of Mexico—a city of five thousand inhabitants, built at the bottom of a deep circular basin, whose rim is only broken on one side by a gash which lets out the waters it collects in the rainy season. Seen from the edge of the basin, just before you commence the descent, a more fantastic picture could scarcely be imagined. The towers of the church are among the tallest in Mexico. During the Fair, the basin is filled to its brim, and a tent-city, containing from three hundred thousand to half a million inhabitants, is planted in it. From Sonora to Oajaca, all Mexico is there, with a good representation from Santa Fé, Texas and California. We descended by a zigzag road, of splendid masonry, crossed the gulley at the bottom by a superb bridge, and stopped at the Diligence Hotel for breakfast. The town was at prayers, on account of cholera. Five hundred people had already died, and the epidemic was just beginning to abate. I saw several of the ignorant populace issue from their huts on their knees, and thus climb their painful way up the hill to the cathedral, saying paternosters as they went. Two attendants went before, spreading sarapes on the stones, to save their knees, and taking them up after they had passed. We ate a hearty breakfast in spite of the terror around us, and resuming our seats in the diligence, were whirled over hill and plain till we saw the beautiful churches of Lagos in the distance. At the hotel, we found the stage from Zacatecas just in, bringing passengers for Mexico.

I took an afternoon stroll through Lagos, visiting the market-place and principal churches, but found nothing worthy of particular note. We arose in the moonlight, chocolated in the *comedor*, or dining-hall, and took our seats—seven in all—in the diligence. We speedily left the neat, gay and pleasant city behind us, and began a journey which promised to be similar to that of the two preceding days—a view of barren table-land, covered with stone fences and cactus hedges, on either side, and blue mountains ever in far perspective. With the sun, however, things looked more cheerful, and soon after entering on the third post, we climbed a stony *cerro*, from which opened a splendid view of the Valley of Leon. Far as the vision extended, the effect was still heightened by a veil of thin blue vapor which arose from the broad leagues of field and meadow below us. In the centre of the picture rose the spires of Villa de Leon, from the midst of green barley-fields and gardens of fruit trees. To the eastward, beyond the valley—which to the south melted into the sky without a barrier—ran the high and rocky ranges of the mineral mountains of Guanajuato. We had nearly crossed the table-land of the Pacific side of Mexico, and these hills were spurs from the spinal ridge of the Continent.

Our horses galloped into Leon—a large and lively town, which pleased me much better than Lagos. We had a capital breakfast of eight courses in the hall of the *Sociedad del Comercio*, and took in two fresh passengers, which just filled the diligence. Dashing out of the town, the road led over the level plain, between fields and gardens of great fertility. In the soft morning light, the animation and beauty of the scene were delightful. The peons were everywhere at work in the fields, watering the trees and vegetables from wells, out of which they drew the water with long poles. At a bridge over the dry bed of a river near the town, I noticed a gang of about fifty ferocious fellows, in ragged sarapes. Several soldiers, well armed, paced up and down the road, and I afterwards learned that the diligence was frequently robbed there. Two long posts down the valley, made with horses going *à carrera*, brought us to Silao. While the grooms were changing teams, we supplied ourselves with oranges, bananas, *zapotes chicos* and *granaditas de China*. The latter fruit is about the size of an egg, with a brittle shell of a bright scarlet color, inside of which is a soft white sack. Breaking this open, the tender, fragrant pulp is revealed—the most dainty, exquisite thing that Nature ever compounded. We also bought an armful of sugar-cane, which we hung on the umbrella-hooks, and chopped up and chewed as thirst required.

From Silao to Guanajuato is but one post. Leaving the former

place, we approached a cape of the mountains, and traveled for
several miles over wild hills covered with immense cactus trees,
the trunks of many of them measuring two feet in diameter.   From
the summit we looked down into a large mountain-basin, opening
towards the south into the Valley of Leon.   On its opposite side,
among mountains whose summits are the more sterile from the
glittering veins of precious ore within, we saw the walls of some of
the mining establishments of Guanajuato.

Of all places in Mexico, the situation of this city is the most
picturesque and remarkable.   It lies like an enchanted city,
buried in the heart of the mountains.   Entering a rocky cañada,
the bottom of which barely affords room for the road, you pass
between high adobe walls, above which, up the steep, rise tier
above tier of blank, windowless, sun-dried houses, looking as if
they had grown out of the earth.   You would take them to be a
sort of cubic chrystalization of the soil.   Every corner in the windings of the road is filled with the buildings of mining companies—
huge fortresses of stone, ramparted as if for defence.   The scene
varies with every moment;—now you look up to a church with
purple dome and painted towers ; now the blank adobe walls, with
here and there a spiry cypress or graceful palm between them,
rise far above you, along the steep ledges of the mountain ; and
again, the mountain itself, with its waste of rock and cactus, is all
you see.   The cañada finally seems to close.   A precipice of
rock—out of a rift in which the stream flows—shuts up the passage.   Ascending this by a twist in the road, you are in the heart
of the city.   Lying partly in the narrow bed of the ravine and
partly on its sides and in its lateral branches, it is only by mount-
ing to some higher eminence that one can realize its extent and
position.   At the farther end of the city the mountains form a

cul de sac. The cañada is a blind passage, and you can only leave it by the road you came. The streets are narrow, crooked, and run up and down in all directions; there is no room for plazas nor alamedas. A little triangular space in front of the cathedral, however, aspires to the former title. The city reminded me of descriptions of the old Moorish towns of Spain—not as they now exist, but as they stood in the fourteenth century.

In the afternoon I took a walk through the city, climbing one of the hills to a cross planted on a small rocky point under the fortress of San Miguel. Thence I could look down on the twisted streets and flat house-tops, and the busy flood of life circulating through all. The churches, with their painted spires and domes, gave a bizarre and picturesque character to the scene. Off to the north, in the sides of the mountains, I could see the entrances to the silver mines, and the villages of the mining communities. Around Guanajuato there are more than a hundred mines, employing about seventy-five thousand workmen. The business of Guanajuato is now very flourishing, the mines having in 1849 yielded $8,400,000, or $600,000 more than the previous year. New mines have been opened on the rich vein of La Luz, which will soon be in a producing state, and promise much higher results. There is a fascination about the business, which is almost equal to that of play. The lucky discoverer of a new mine will frequently squander away the sudden wealth he has acquired in a week's dissipation. The wages of the common workmen vary from four reals to two dollars a day.

Before night I visited the cathedral and the churches of San Diego and San Felipe—the latter a dark old structure, covered with quaint, half-Gothic ornaments, its front shaded by several tall cypresses. In the church of San Diego, I saw a picture of great beauty, of the Murillo school, but hardly, I think, an original of the renowned master of Spanish painting. After dinner, while wandering about, looking at the fruit-stands, which were lighted with a red glow by smoky torches, I witnessed a curious ceremony. One of a band of robbers, who had been taken and convicted, was to be shot the next morning. All the bells in the city commenced tolling at sunset, and the incessant ding-dong they kept up for nearly two hours, was enough to drive one frantic. I heard the sound of music, and saw the twinkling of wax tapers ; I therefore pressed through the crowd into the middle of the little plaza, to obtain a good view of the procession. First came a company of soldiers, with a military band, playing dirges ; after this the Bishop of the city bearing the Host, under a canopy of white and silver, borne by priests, who also carried lanterns of blue glass ; another company of soldiers followed, and after them a long double line of citizens, each of whom held an immense burning taper in his hand. With the clang of bells and the wail of brazen instruments, they came towards us. The thousands in the plaza dropped on their knees, leaving me standing alone in the centre. A moment's reflection convinced me of the propriety of following their example, so I sank down between a woman with a very dirty rebosa and a black-bearded fellow, who might have been the comrade of the condemned robber.

The procession, keeping a slow and measured pace, proceeded to the prison, where the sacrament of extreme unction was administered to the criminal. It then returned to the cathedral, which was brilliantly lighted, and filled with a dense throng of people. The military band was stationed in the centre, under the dome, and mingled its harmonies with those of the powerful organ. I could get no further than the door-way, whence the whole interior was visible as a lighted picture, framed in the gloomy arch under which I stood. The rise and swell of the choral voices—the deep, stunning peal of the bells in the tower—the solemn attitude of the crowd, and the blaze of light under which all these imposing ceremonies were seen—made a powerful impression on me. The people about me constantly repeated their paternosters, and seemed to feel a deep sympathy with the convicted. I remembered, that in the afternoon I had seen in the cathedral a man somewhat advanced in years, who was praying with an intensity of grief and supplication that made him for the time insensible to all else. His sobs and groans were so violent as to shake his whole frame ; I had never seen a more vehement expression of anguish. Thinking he might have been the robber's father, I began to have some compassion for the former, though now and then a wicked feeling of rejoicing would steal in, that another of the tribe was soon to be exterminated. The most curious feature of the scene was a company of small boys, carrying bundles of leaves on which was printed the " Last Dying Speech and Confession," in poetry, the burden being " *Adios, Guanajuato amado !*" These boys were scattered through the crowd, crying out : " Here you have my sentence, my confession, my death, my farewell to Guanajuato —all for a *cuartilla !*" The exercises were kept up so long, that finally I grew weary, and went to bed, where the incessant bells rang death-knells in my dreams.

In Guanajuato I tasted *pulque* for the first and last time. Seeing a woman at the corner of a street with several large jars of what I took to be barley-water, I purchased a glass. I can only liken the taste of this beverage to a distillation of sour milk (if there could be such a thing) strongly tinctured with cayenne pepper and hartshorn. Men were going about the streets with cans on their heads, containing ices made from tropical fruits, which were much more palatable.

They even have authors in Guanajuato. On the theatre bills I saw the announcement that an original tragedy entitled " *El Amor Conyugal*," by a young Guanajuatense, was in preparation. " The precious comedy of the Two Fernandos and the Two Pepas" was to be given as an afterpiece—probably a travesty of the " Comedy of Errors."

CHAPTER XV.

WE were roused in Guanajuato at three o'clock in the morning, for the *jornada* of one hundred and ten miles to Queretaro. A splendid moon was riding near the zenith, with her attendant star at her side; and by her light we drove down the ominous depths of the cañada. The clumsy leaves of the cactus, along the ledges of the hills, seemed in the uncertain light, like the heads of robbers peering over the rocks; the crosses of the dead, here and there, spread out their black arms, and we were not free from all apprehensions of attack, until, after a post of three leagues, we reached the level and secure land of the *Bajio*. Once, only, a company of about twenty wild-looking men, whose weapons glittered in the moonlight, hooted at us as we passed; we took them to be a part of the robber-band, on their way to Guanajuato to witness the execution of their comrade.

In five posts we reached the city of Salamanca, where breakfast was already on the table. No sooner had the final dish of frijoles and cup of coffee been dispatched, than the *cochero* summoned us. The mozo drew away with a jerk the rope which held the four leaders; the horses plunged and pranced till the lumbering mass of the diligence began to move, when they set off in a furious gallop. For ten miles, over the level road, the speed was scarcely slackened, till we drew up at the next post, and exchanged our dusty and reeking steeds for a fresh team, as fiery and furious as the first.

The country through which we passed, is one of the richest regions in Mexico. It is called the *Bajio*, or Lowland, but is in fact an extent of table-land, about four thousand feet above the level of the sea, and only lower than the mountain-ridges which enclose it and draw from the upper clouds the streams that give it perpetual growth. From the city of Leon, near Lagos, it extends to San Juan del Rio, beyond Queretaro—a distance of nearly two hundred miles. It is traversed by the Rio Lerma, the stream which, rising in the Volcano of Toluca (the neighbor of Popocatapetl) mingles with the waters of Lake Chapala, and afterwards—first as the Rio Blanco and then as the Rio Santiago—finds its way into the Pacific at San Blas. This immense level is all under fine cultivation and covered with thousand-acre fields of wheat, maize and barley in different stages of growth. The white fronts of haciendas gleamed from out their embowering gardens, in the distance, and the spires of the country towns, rising at intervals, gave life and animation to the picture. In the afternoon we passed the city of Zelaya, nearly smothered in clouds of dust that rose from the dry soil.

As we reached the boundary of the State of Queretaro, eight lancers, armed likewise with escopettes and holster-pistols, galloped out of the cactus on a wild, stony hill, and took their places on each side of us. They constituted a military escort (at the expense of the passengers,) to the gates of Queretaro. With their red pennons fluttering in the wind and their rugged little horses spurred into a gallop, they were very picturesque objects. Our time was divided in watching their movements and looking out for the poles planted by the roadside as a sign that robbers had been taken and shot there. My Mexican fellow-travelers pointed to these tokens of unscrupulous punishment with evident satisfaction. A large tree near Queretaro, with a great many lateral branches, bears a sign with the words "*Por Ladrones*," (For Robbers,) in large letters. It is probably used when a whole company is caught at once.

We drove into Queretaro after dark, and the only glimpse I had of the place was from the balcony of the hotel. I regretted not having arrived earlier, for the purpose of visiting the cotton manufactory of Don Gaetano Rubio, which is the largest in the Republic. Among the passengers in the diligence from Mexico, who joined us at the dinner-table, was a jovial padre, who talked constantly of the Monplaisir troupe of dancers and Cœnen, the violinist. In fact, he was more familiar with American and European theatricals than any one I had met for a long time, and gave me a ready account of the whereabouts of Cerito, Ellsler, Taglioni, and all the other divinities of the dance. He then commenced a dissertation upon the character of the different modern languages. The English, he said, was the language of commerce; the French, of conversation; the German, of diplomacy, because there were no words of double meaning in it!—and the Spanish, of devotion. With his conversation and delightful cigaritos, I passed the hour before bed-time very pleasantly. I never met a more lively and entertaining padre.

We drove to the town of San Juan del Rio, eleven leagues distant, for breakfast. A fresh escort was given us at every post, for which a fresh contribution of two reals was levied on each passenger. Towards evening, leaving the *Bajio*, we came upon a

large, arid *llano*, flat as a table, and lying at the foot of the
Mount of Capulalpan. A string of mules, carrying stone from the
mountains, stretched across it, till they almost vanished in the
perspective. One by one they came up out of the distance, emptied the stones, which were heaped upon their backs in rough
wicker frames, and turned about to repeat the journey. They
belonged to the estate of Señor Zurutuza, proprietor of the diligence lines of Mexico, who shows as much prudence and skill in
the cultivation of his lands as in the arrangement of his stages
and hotels. The estate which he purchased of the Mexican
Government, at a cost of $300,000, contains thirty-seven square
leagues, nearly all of which is arable land. The buildings stand
in a little valley, nine thousand feet above the sea. The principal
storehouse is two hundred feet square, and solid as a fortress. An
arched entrance, closed by massive gates, leads to a paved court-
yard, around which runs a lofty gallery, with pillars of oak resting
on blocks of lava. Under this shelter were stored immense piles
of wheat and chopped straw. On the outside, a number of persons were employed in removing the grain from a large circular
floor of masonry, where it had been trodden out by mules, and
separating it from the chaff by tossing it diligently in the wind.
The hotel for the accommodation of travelers, is a new and elegant structure, and a decided improvement on other buildings of
the kind in Mexico.

We slept soundly in the several rooms allotted to us, and by
daybreak next morning were on the summit of the Pass of Capulalpan, about eleven thousand feet above the sea. The air was
thin and cold ; the timber was principally oak, of a stunted and
hardy kind, and the general appearance of the place is desolate in
the extreme. Here, where the streams of the two oceans are

divided, the first view of Popocatapetl, at more than a hundred miles distance, greets the traveler. A descent of many miles, through splendid plantations, lying in the lap of the mountains, brought us to the old town of Tula, on the banks of the Tula River, which empties into the Gulf, at Tampico. Here we breakfasted, and then started on our last stage towards the capital. Crossing a low range of hills, we reached the Desagua, an immense canal, cut for the draining of the Valley of Mexico. The afternoon was hot and breezeless; clouds of dust enveloped and almost stifled us, rising as they rolled away till they looked like slender pillars, swayed from side to side by the vibrations of the air. We passed the towns of Guatitlan and Tanepantla, where we only stopped to get a drink of *tepache*, a most nourishing and refreshing beverage, compounded of parched corn, pineapple, and sugar. The road was hedged by immense aloes, some of which had leaves ten feet in length: they are cultivated in great quantities for the pulque, which is manufactured from their juice. A few hours of this travel, on the level floor of the Valley of Mexico, brought us to the suburbs, where we met scores of people in carriages and on horseback, going out to take their evening *paseo* around the Alameda. Rattling over the streets of the spacious capital, in a few minutes we were brought to a stand in the yard of the Casa de Diligencias.

A few minutes after my arrival, the Vera Cruz stage drove into the yard. The first person who jumped out was my friend Mr. Parrot, U. S. Consul at Mazatlan. Gov. Letcher, our Envoy to Mexico, came in the same stage, but was met at the Peñon Grande by a number of Americans in carriages, and brought into the city. It is a pleasant thing to have friends of your own size. I made my first appearance in the City of the Montezumas covered with dust and clad in the weather-beaten corduroys, which were all the robbers left me. Thanks to the kind offer of Mr. Parrot and Mr. Peyton, who accompanied him, I sat down to dinner in half an hour afterwards, looking and feeling much more like a member of civilized society.

CHAPTER XVI.

SCENES IN THE MEXICAN CAPITAL.

I SALLIED out, on the bright sunny morning after reaching Mexico, to make a survey of the city. The sky was cloudless except on the horizon, in the direction of Popocatapetl, and the air was charmingly cool and fresh. Its rarity, by accelerating the breathing, had a stimulating effect, but I found that a faster pace than ordinary exhausted me in a few minutes. Most of the shops were closed, and the people from the neighboring villages began to come in for the morning mass. The streets are broad, tolerably clean, and have an air of solidity and massive strength beyond that of any modern city. The houses are all of stone, with few windows on the streets, but an arched gateway in the centre, leading to a patio, or courtyard, where the only correct view of their size and magnificence may be obtained. The glimpses through these gateways, while passing, are often very beautiful—the richly-sculptured frame of stone enclosing a sunny picture of a fountain, a cluster of orange-trees, or the slender, graceful arches of the corridor. The buildings are painted of some light, fresh color, pink and white being predominant; some of them, indeed, are entirely covered with arabesque patterns in fresco. The streets run at right angles, with nearly Philadelphian

7*

regularity, but the system of naming them is very confusing to a stranger. A name extends no farther than a single block, the same street having sometimes as many as twenty different names in different places. Thus, while there are several thousand names of streets in the city, (all of them long and difficult to remember) the actual number of streets is small.

I wandered about for some time, looking for the Grand Plaza, and at last fell into the wake of the mass-going crowd, as the surest way to find it. It is in the very centre of the city, though the business quarter lies almost entirely on the western side. It is one of the most imposing squares in the world, and still far inferior to what it might be made. It covers about fourteen.acres, which are entirely open and unbroken, except by a double row of orange-trees in front of the Cathedral. The splendid equestrian statue of Charles IV. by the sculptor Tolsa, which formerly stood in the centre, has been removed since the war of Independence, and the Government has never been able to replace it by something more to its republican taste. The National Palace, with a front of five hundred feet, occupies nearly the entire eastern side of the plaza, while the Cathedral, with a church adjoining, fills the northern. Around the other sides runs a *cortal*, whose arches are nearly blocked up by the wares and gay fabrics there disposed for sale. One of the houses forming this cortal was built by Cortez, and is still owned by his descendants. As in our own cities, there is a row of hacks strung along one side of the plaza, the drivers of which assail you with continual invitations to ride.

The Cathedral is grand and impressive from its very size, but the effect of the front is greatly injured by its incongruous style of architecture. There seems to have been no single design adopted, but after half had been built, the architect changed his plan and finished the remainder in a different style. The front, as high as the Cathedral roof, has a venerable appearance of age and neglect, while the two massive, square, unadorned towers rising from it, are as brilliantly white and fresh as if erected yesterday. The front of the church adjoining is embossed with very elaborate ornaments of sculpture, all showing the same disregard of architectural unity. The interior of the Cathedral is far more perfect in its structure. The nave, resting its lofty arch on pillars of a semi-Gothic character, with the gorgeous pile of the high-altar at its extremity, blazing with gold and silver and precious marbles, looks truly sublime in the dim, subdued light which fills it. The railing around the altar is solid silver, as well as the lamps which burn before it. In the shrines along the side aisles there are many paintings of fine character, but everywhere the same flash of gold and appearance of lavish treasure. The Cathedral was crowded to the very door by a throng of rancheros, Indians, stately ladies in silks and jewels, soldiers and *lepéros*, kneeling side by side. The sound of the organ, bearing on its full flood the blended voices of the choir, pealed magnificently through the nave. There were some very fine voices among the singers, but their performance was wanting in the grand and perfect unison which distinguishes the Italian chorus.

In the afternoon, there was a great fair or festival at Tacubaya, and half the population of the city went out to attend it. The stages in front of the Diligence Hotel, which bore the inscription on their sides: " *A Tacubaya, por 2 reales*," were jammed with passengers. I preferred a quiet walk in the Alameda to a suffocating ride in the heat and dust, and so did my friend, Peyton. The Alameda is a charming place, completely shaded by tall trees, and musical with the plash of fountains.

Through its long avenues of foliage, the gay equipages of the
aristocracy may be seen rolling to and from the *paseo*—President
Herrera, in a light, open carriage, followed by a guard of honor,
among them. We roamed through the cool, shaded walks, finding sufficient amusement in the curious groups and characters we
constantly met until the afternoon shadows grew long and the sun
had nearly touched the Nevada of Toluca. Then, joining the increasing crowd, we followed the string of carriages past a guard-
house where a company of trumpeters shattered all the surround-
ing air by incessant prolonged blasts, that nearly tore up the
paving-stones. A beautiful road, planted with trees, and flanked
by convenient stone benches, extended beyond for about a mile,
having a circle at its further end, around which the carriages
passed, and took their stations in the return line. We sat down
on one of the benches facing the ring, enjoying the tranquillity of
the sunset and the animation of the scene before us. The towers
of Mexico rose behind us, above the gardens which belt the city;
the rock of Chapultepec was just visible in front, and far to the
south-east, a snowy glimmer, out of the midst of a pile of clouds,
revealed the cone of Popocatapetl. Among the equipages were
some of great magnificence : that of Don Gaetano Rubio was
perhaps the most costly. Large American horses are in great
demand for these displays, and a thousand dollars a pair is frequently paid for them. The mixture of imported vehicles—English, French and American—with the bomb-proof arks and move-
able fortifications of the country, was very amusing, though their
contrast was not more marked than that of the occupants. The
great ambition of a Mexican family is to ride in a carriage on all
public occasions, and there are hundreds who starve themselves

on tortillas and deny themselves every comfort but the cigarito, that they may pay the necessary hire.

I went one evening to the Teatro de Santa Anna, which is one of the finest theatres in the world. On this occasion, the performance might have honorably stood the ordeal of even Paris criticism. There was a ballet by the Monplaisir troupe, songs by the prima donna of the native opera and violin solos by Franz Coenen. The theatre is very large, having, if I remember rightly, five tiers of boxes, yet it was crowded in every part. There was a great display of costly dresses and jewelry, but I saw much less beauty than on the moonlit plaza of Guadalajara. The tendency of the Mexican women to corpulency very soon destroys the bloom and graces of youth ; indeed, their season of beauty is even more brief than in the United States. Between the acts the spectators invariably fell to smoking. The gentlemen lit their *puros*, the ladies produced their delicate boxes of cigaritos and their matches, and for some minutes after the curtain fell, there was a continual snapping and fizzing of brimstone all over the house. By the time the curtain was ready to rise, the air was sensibly obscured, and the chandeliers glimmered through a blue haze. At home, this habit of smoking by the ladies is rather graceful and pretty ; the fine paper cigar is handled with an elegance that shows off the little arts and courtesies of Spanish character, with the same effect as a fan or a bouquet ; but a whole congregation of women smoking together, I must admit, did take away much of the reverence with which we are wont to regard the sex. Because a lady may be a Juno in beauty, is no reason why she should thus retire into a cloud—nor is the odor of stale tobacco particularly Olympian.

The streets of Mexico are always an interesting study. Even

after visiting the other large cities of the Republic, one is here introduced to new and interesting types of Mexican humanity. Faces of the pure Aztec blood are still to be found in the squares and market-places, and the canal which joins Lakes Chalco and Tezcuco is filled with their flat canoes, laden with fruits, vegetables and flowers. They have degenerated in everything but their hostility to the Spanish race, which is almost as strong as in the days of Montezuma. The *léperos* constitute another and still more disgusting class; no part of the city is free from them. They implore you for alms with bended knees and clasped hands, at every turn; they pick your pockets in broad daylight, or snatch away your cloak if there is a good opportunity; and if it be an object with any one to have you removed from this sphere of being, they will murder you for a small consideration. The second night I spent in Mexico, my pocket was picked in the act of passing a corner where two or three of them were standing in a group. I discovered the loss before I had gone ten steps further; but, though I turned immediately, there was no one to be seen. The *aguadores*, or water-carriers, are another interesting class, as they go about with heavy earthen jars suspended on their backs by a band about the forehead, and another smaller jar swinging in front to balance it, by a band over the top of the head. The priests, in their black cassocks and shovel hats with brims a yard long, are curious figures; the monasteries in the city send out large numbers of fat and sensual friars, whose conduct even in public is a scandal to the respectable part of the community. In all the features of its out-door life, Mexico is quite as motley and picturesque as any of the old cities of Spain. The Republic seems to have in no way changed the ancient order, except by tearing down all the emblems of royalty and substituting the eagle and cactus in their stead.

The scarcity of all antiquities of the Aztec race, will strike travelers who visit the city. Not one stone of the ancient capital has been left upon another, while, by the gradual recession of the waters of the lakes, the present Mexico, though built precisely on the site of the ancient one, stands on dry ground. There are frequently inundations, it is true, caused by long-continued rains, which the mountain slopes to the north-east and south-west send into the valley, but the construction of the Desagua—an immense canal connecting Lake Tezcuco with the Rio Montezuma—has greatly lessened the danger. Of all the temples, palaces, and public edifices of the Aztecs, the only remains are the celebrated Calendar, built into one corner of the cathedral, the Sacrificial Stone and a collection of granite gods in the National Museum. The Calendar is an immense circular stone, probably ten feet in diameter, containing the divisions of the Aztec year, and the astronomical signs used by that remarkable people. The remaining antiquities are piled up neglectedly in the court-yard of the Museum, where the stupid natives come to stare at them, awed, yet apparently fascinated by their huge, terrible features. The Sacrificial Stone is in perfect preservation. It is like a great mill-stone of some ten or twelve feet diameter, with a hollow in the centre, from which a groove slants to the edge, to carry away the blood of the victim. Scattered around it on the pavement were idols of all grotesque forms, feathered serpents and hideous combinations of human and animal figures. The Aztec war-god, Quetzalcoatl, was the hugest and most striking of all. He was about fourteen feet in height, with four faces, and as many pairs of arms and legs, fronting towards the quarters of the compass ; his mouth was open and tongue projecting, and in the hollow thus formed, the heart of the victim was thrust, while yet warm and palpitating. His grim features struck me with awe and something like terror, when I thought of the thousands of human hearts that had stained his insatiate tongues. Here, at least, the Aztecs had a truer conception of the Spirit of War than ourselves. We still retain the Mars of the poetic Greeks—a figure of strength and energy, and glorious ardor only—not the grand monster which all barbaric tribes, to whom war is a natural instinct, build for their worship.

There are some relics of the Spanish race in this museum, which I should not omit to mention. In one dusty corner, behind a little wooden railing, are exhibited the coats-of-mail of Cortez and Alvarado. The great Cortez, to judge from his helmet, breast-plate and cuishes, was a short, broad-chested and powerful man—the very build for daring and endurance. Alvarado was a little taller and more slight, which may account for his celebrated leap—the measure of which is still shown on a wall near the city, though the ditch is filled up. In the centre of the court-yard stands the celebrated equestrian statue of Charles IV., by the Mexican sculptor, Tolsa. It is of bronze, and colossal size. In the general spirit and forward action of the figures, it is one of the best equestrian statues in the world. The horse, which was modeled from an Andalusian stallion of pure blood, has been censured. It differs, in fact, very greatly from the perfect Grecian model, especially in the heavy chest and short round flank ; but those who have seen the Andalusian horse consider it a perfect type of that breed. It is a work in which Mexico may well glory, for any country might be proud to have produced it.

CHAPTER XVII.

MEXICAN POLITICS AND POLITICAL MEN.

I SPENT one morning during my stay in Mexico, in visiting both Houses of the Mexican Congress, which were then in session, in the National Palace. I could not but regret, on approaching this edifice, that so fine an opportunity for architectural effect had been lost through a clumsy and incongruous plan of building. The front of five hundred feet, had it been raised another story, and its flat pink surface relieved by a few simple pilasters and cornices, would have equaled that of the Pitti Palace or the Royal *Residenz* in Munich. One of its court-yards, with a fountain in the centre and double gallery running around the four sides, is nevertheless complete and very beautiful. While looking out of the windows of the Palace on the magnificent square, the foremost picture in my mind's eye was not that of Cortez and Alvarado, battling their way back to Tlascala, after the " Noche Triste ;" not that of the splendid trains of the Viceroys of yet powerful Spain; but the triumphal entry of Scott, when the little army that had fought its way in from Chapultepec, greeted his appearance on the Plaza with huzzas that brought tears even into Mexican eyes. Think as one may of the character of the war, there are scenes in it which stir the blood and brighten the eye.

Mr. Belden, an American many years resident in Mexico, accompanied me to the Halls of Congress, and pointed out the principal characters present. We first visited the Senate Chamber—a small elliptical room in the centre of the Palace. There were no desks except for the Secretaries, the members being seated on a continuous bench, which ran around the room, with a rail in front of it. Probably two-thirds of the Senators—fifteen or twenty in all—were present. The best head among them is that of Otero, who, I think, was one of the Cabinet during the war. He is a large, strongly-built man, with features expressing not only intelligence, but power. At the end of the room sat Don Luis Cuevas, one of the Commissioners who signed the Treaty of Guadalupe Hidalgo—a man of polished bearing, and, from appearance, something of a *diplomat*. Gen. Almonte, whose low forehead, broad cheek-bones and dark skin betray his Indian blood, occupied the seat next to Pedraza, the President of a few days during a revolution in 1828. Almonte is the son of the Liberator Morelos, and that circumstance alone gave him an interest in my eyes.

The demeanor of the Senate is exceedingly quiet and grave. The speeches are short, though not, in consequence, always to the point. On the contrary, I am told that any definite action on any subject is as difficult to be had as in our own Congress. It is better, however, to do nothing decorously, than after a riotous fashion.

The Hall of Congress fronts on one of the inner courts of the Palace. It is semi-circular in form, and lighted by windows of blue glass, near the top. As in the Senate, the members have no desks, but are ranged along two semi-circular benches, the outer one raised a step from the floor. The Speaker sits on a broad platform, in front of the centre of the chord, with two Secretaries on each hand. At each corner of the platform is a circular pulpit, just large enough to take in a spare man nearly to the armpits. They are used by the members for set harangues. Behind the Speaker's chair, and elevated above it, is a sort of throne with two seats, under a crimson canopy. Here, the President of the Republic and the Speaker of Congress take their seats, at the opening and close of each Session. Above the canopy, in a gilded frame, on a ground of the Mexican tricolor, hangs the sword of Iturbide. A picture of the Virgin of Guadalupe, with her blue mantle and silver stars, completes the decorations. Around the architrave of the pillars which form the semi-circle and across the cornice of the chord, are inscribed, in letters of gold, the names of the Mexican Chiefs of the War of Independence—conspicuous among them those of Morelos, Bravo, Victoria and Mina.

The Mexican Congress elects its Speaker monthly. The incumbent at the time, Portillo, was a young man, who presided with admirable dignity and decorum. As in the Senate, the members exhibit a grave and courteous demeanor ; the etiquette of dignified legislation, I presume, is never violated. The only notable Representative present was Arrangoiz, whose name is well known in the United States. I was disappointed in not seeing Alaman, the head of the Monarchist faction, Editor of the *Universal*, and author of an excellent History of Mexico, then in the course of publication. Two or three short speeches were made during my visit, but I was not sufficiently versed either in the language or politics, to get more than the general drift of them. Congress appeared to be doing nothing satisfactory ; the thinking population (a very small number) were discontented, and with reason. A short time previous, the Report of the Committee of Finance came up for discussion. After engaging the House for several days, during which many warm speeches were made on both sides, all seemed ready for a decision ; when, lo ! the members suddenly determined that *they had no right to vote upon it !*

One o'clock the same afternoon was the hour appointed for the presentation of Mr. Letcher, the new Envoy from the United States. On coming out of the Senate Chamber we noticed that the corridor leading to the rooms of the President was deserted by the groups of officers in full uniform who had been lounging about the door. Entering the ante-chamber, we found that Mr. Letcher, with Mr. Walsh, Secretary of Legation, had just passed into the Hall of Audience. Mr. Belden was well known to all the officers of Government, and his company procured us admission at once. We took our places among the Secretaries of the different Departments, about half way up the Hall. Gen. Herrera, the President, was seated on a platform at the end of the room; under a crimson canopy, having on his right hand Lacunza, Minister of Foreign Affairs, and on his left Castañeda, Minister of Justice. The other Ministers, with a number of officers of the General Staff, were ranged at the foot of the platform. Mr. Letcher had just commenced his address as we entered. He appeared slightly embarrassed during the first phrases, but soon recovered the proper composure. I had no doubt, however, that he would have felt much more at home in making a stump speech in his native Kentucky. His address consisted mainly of expressions of good will on the part of the United States, and a desire for more intimate and amicable relations between the two Governments. Gen. Herrera, on receiving the letters accrediting Mr. Letcher, replied in a neat speech, cordially responding to the expressions of amity which had been made, and invoking for both nations the same harmony in their mutual relations as they already possessed in their constitutional forms.

After the interchange of a few compliments, Mr. Letcher took his leave, and immediately afterwards the President rose and left the hall, in company with his Ministers. He bowed to us in passing, probably recognizing us as Americans. He is a man of about sixty, of short stature, and with a countenance whose prominent expression is honesty and benevolence. This corresponds with the popular idea of his character. He is a man of excellent heart, but lacks energy and determination. His Government, though quiet and peaceful enough at present, is not sufficiently strong for Mexico. So long as the several States continue to defy and violate the Federal Compact, a powerful Head is needed to the General Government. The rule of Herrera met with no open opposition. At the time of my visit, the country was perfectly quiet. The insurrection in the Sierra Madre had been entirely quelled, and the ravages of the Indians in Durango and Chihuahua appeared to have subsided for a time. Nevertheless, the Conservative party, whose tendency is towards a monarchy, was said to be on the increase—a fact no doubt attributable to the influence and abilities of Alaman, its avowed leader. The name of Santa Anna had been brought forward by his friends, as a candidate for Congress from the district of the Capital, though his success was scarcely a matter of hope.

The Government was still deeply embarrassed by its forced loans, and Congress took the very worst means to settle its difficulty. A committee, appointed to report some plan of settlement, made the following propositions, which I here give, as a curiosity in legislation :—1. That the Government be authorized to make an amicable arrangement with its creditors, within the space of

forty days. (!) 2. That such arrangement cannot take effect
without the approbation of Congress; (!!) and 3. That the Government be authorized to accept a further sum of $300,000 on
the American indemnity. The resignation of Señor Elorriaga,
the Minister of Finance, was fully expected, and took place, in
fact, about three weeks after I left. Very few Ministers hold this
office more than two or three months. The entire want of confidence between the Executive and Legislative Departments utterly
destroys the efficiency of the Mexican Government. The Ministers wear a chain, which is sometimes so shortened by the caprice
of Congress, that the proper exercise of their functions is rendered
impossible.

Several of the States had a short time previous been taking
singular liberties with the Constitution. For instance, the Legis-
latures of Zacatecas, Durango and Jalisco, had separately passed
laws regulating the revenue not only on internal commerce, but
foreign imports! The duties on many articles were enormous,
as, for instance, in the State of Jalisco, 37 1-2 cents per lb. on
tobacco, and 75 cents on snuff. Zacatecas, with a curious dis-
crimination, imposed a duty of 12 1-2 per cent. on home manufactures, and 5 per cent. on foreign merchandise! In such a
state of things one knows not which most to wonder at, the
audacity of the States, or the patient sufferance of the Supreme
Government.

I scanned with some curiosity the faces and forms of the chief
officers of the Republic as they passed.

Herrera wore the uniform of a general—a more simple costume
than that of the other officers present, whose coats were orna-
mented with red facings and a profusion of gold embroidery. The
Ministers, except Arista, were dressed in plain suits of black.

Lacunza is a man of low stature and dark complexion, and a barely perceptible cast of shrewdness is mingled with the natural intelligence of his features. Castañeda, on the other hand, is tall, thin, with a face of which you are certain, at the first glance, that it knows how to keep its owner's secrets. The finest-looking man present was Gen. Arista, who is six feet high, and stout in proportion, with a large head, light hair closely cropped, fair complexion and gray eyes. From the cast of his features, one would take him to be a great overgrown Scotch boy, who had somehow blundered into a generalship. He is said to have the most influential hand in the Cabinet. Among the States of the North there is, as is well known, a powerful party devoted to his interests.

While in Mexico, I had the pleasure of meeting with Don Vicente Garcia Torres, the talented editor of the *Monitor Republicano*, as well as with several of the writers for *El Siglo Diez y Nueve*. To M. Réné Masson, the enterprising editor and proprietor of *Le Trait D'Union*, (the only foreign journal in Mexico,) I was also indebted for many courteous attentions. His paper is conducted with more industry and gives a more intelligible view of Mexican affairs than any of the native prints. The Count de la Cortina, the most accomplished writer in Mexico, and author of several works, was pointed out to me in the street one day. He possesses a princely fortune and the finest picture-gallery in America.

CHAPTER XVIII.

RIDES TO CHAPULTEPEC AND GUADALUPE.

No American, whatever be his moral creed or political sentiments, should pass through Mexico without a visit to the battle-fields in the Valley, where his country's arms obtained such signal triumphs. To me they had a more direct, thrilling interest than the remains of Aztec Empire or the Spanish Viceroyalty. I was fortunate in seeing them with a companion, to whom every rood of ground was familiar, and who could trace all the operations of Scott's army, from San Augustin to the Grand Plaza in the city. We started for Chapultepec one fine afternoon, with Mr. Belden, taking his carriage and span of black mules. We drove first to the Garita de Belén, where one of the aqueducts enters the city. Here a strong barricade was carried after the taking of Chapultepec by Pillow's division, while Worth, following down the line of the other aqueduct, got possession of the Garita de San Cosmé. The brick arches are chipped with shot, for the whole distance of three miles. The American troops advanced by springing from arch to arch, being exposed, as they approached the Garita, to a cross-fire from two batteries. The running battle of the Aqueducts, from Chapultepec to Mexico, a distance of three miles, was a brilliant achievement, and had not our forces been so flushed and excited with the storming of the height, and the spirit of the Mexicans proportionately lessened, the slaughter must have been terrible.

We followed the aqueduct, looking through its arches on the green wheat-fields of the Valley, the shining villages in the distance and sometimes the volcanoes, as the clouds grew thinner about their white summits. At last, we reached the gate of Chapultepec. Mr. Belden was known to the officer on guard, and we passed unchallenged into the shade of Montezuma's cypresses. Chapultepec is a volcanic hill, probably two hundred feet in height, standing isolated on the level floor of the valley. Around its base is the grove of cypress trees, known as Montezuma's Garden—great, gnarled trunks, which have been formed by the annual rings of a thousand years, bearing aloft a burden of heavy and wide-extending boughs, with venerable beards of gray moss. The changeless black-green of the foliage, the dull, wintry hue of the moss, and the gloomy shadows which always invest this grove, spoke to me more solemnly of the Past—of ancient empire, now overthrown, ancient splendor, now fallen into dust, and ancient creeds now forgotten and contemned,—than the shattered pillars of the Roman Forum or the violated tombs of Etruria. I saw them on a shaded, windless day, with faint glimmerings of sunshine between the black and heavy masses of cloud. The air was so still that not a filament of the long mossy streamers trembled ; the trees stood like giant images of bronze around the rocky foot of the hill. The father of the band, who, like a hoary-headed seneschal, is stationed at the base of the ascending carriage-way, measures forty-five feet in circumference, and there are in the grove several others of dimensions but little inferior. The first

8

onset of our troops, in storming Chapultepec, was made under cover of these trees.

Leaving our carriage and mules in charge of the old cypress, we climbed the hill on foot. The zigzag road still retains its embankment of adobes and the small corner-batteries thrown up in anticipation of the attack ; the marks of the cannon-balls from Tacubaya and the high ground behind Molino del Rey, are everywhere visible. The fortress on the summit of Chapultepec has been for many years used as a National Military Academy. We found a company of the cadets playing ball on a graveled terrace in front of the entrance. One of them escorted us to the private apartments of the commanding officer, which are built along the edge of a crag, on the side towards Mexico. Mr. Belden was well acquainted with the officer, but, unfortunately, he was absent. His wife, however, received us with great courtesy and sent for one of the Lieutenants attached to the Academy. A splendid Munich telescope was brought from the observatory, and we adjourned to the balcony for a view of the Valley of Mexico.

I wish there was a perspective in words—something beyond the mere suggestiveness of sound—some truer representative of color, and light, and grand aerial distance ; for I scarcely know how else to paint the world-wide panorama spread around me. Chapultepec, as I have said before, stands isolated in the centre of the Valley. The mountains of Toluca approach to within fifteen miles beyond Tacubaya, and the island-like hills of Guadalupe are not very distant, on the opposite side ; but in nearly every other direction the valley fades away for fifty or sixty miles before striking the foot of the mountains. The forms of the chains which wall in this little world are made irregular and wonderfully picturesque by the embaying curves of the Valley—now receding far and faint,

now piled nearer in rugged and barren grandeur, now tipped with
a spot of snow, like the Volcano of Toluca, or shooting far into
the sky a dazzling cone, like cloud-girdled Popocatapel. But
the matchless Valley—how shall I describe that ? How reflect on
this poor page its boundless painting of fields and gardens, its silvery plantations of aloes, its fertilizing canals, its shimmering
lakes, embowered villages and convents, and the many-towered capital in the centre—the boss of its great enameled shield ? Before us
the aqueducts ran on their thousand arches towards the city, the
water sparkling in their open tops ; the towers of the cathedral,
touched with a break of sunshine shone white as silver against the
cloud-shadowed mountains ; Tacubaya lay behind, with its palaces
and gardens ; farther to the north Tacuba, with the lone cypress
of the " Noche Triste," and eastward, on the point of a mountain-
cape shooting out towards Lake Tezcuco, we saw the shrine of
Our Lady of Guadalupe. Around the foot of our rocky watch-
tower, we looked down on the heads of the cypresses, out of whose
dark masses it seemed to rise, sundered by that weird ring from
the warmth and light and beauty of the far-reaching valley-world.

We overlooked all the battle-grounds of the Valley, but I felt
a hesitancy at first in asking the Lieutenant to point out the localities. Mr. Belden at length asked whether we could see the
height of Padierna, or the *pedregal* (field of lava) which lies to
the left of it. The officer immediately understood our wish, and
turning the glass first upon the Peñon Grande, (an isolated hill
near Ayotla,) traced the march of Gen. Scott's army around Lake
Chalco to the town of San Augustin, near which the first hostilities
commenced. We could see but a portion of the field of Padierna,
more familiarly known as Contreras. It lies on the lower slopes
of the Nevada of Toluca, and overlooking the scenes of the subse-

quent actions. The country is rough and broken, and the crossing of the famed *pedregal*, from the far glimpse I had of the
ground, must have been a work of great labor and peril. Nearly
east of this, on the dead level of the valley, is the memorable field
of Churubusco. The *tête de pont*, where the brunt of the battle
took place, was distinctly visible, and I could count every tree in
the gardens of the convent. The panic of the Mexicans on the
evening after the fight at Churubusco was described to me as having been without bounds. Foreigners residing in the capital say
it might then have been taken with scarce a blow.

Beyond Tacubaya, we saw the houses of Miscoac, where the
army was stationed for some time before it advanced to the former
place. Gen. Scott's head-quarters was in the Bishop's Palace at
Tacubaya, which is distinctly seen from Chapultepec and within
actual reach of its guns. On an upland slope north of the village
and towards Tacuba the shattered walls of the Casa Mata were
pointed out. Near at hand—almost at the very base of the
hill—rose the white gable of Molino del Rey. The march of the
attacking lines could be as distinctly traced as on a map. How
Chapultepec, which commands every step of the way, could be
stormed and carried with such a small force, seems almost miraculous. Persons who witnessed the affair from Tacubaya told me
that the yells of the American troops as they ascended the hill in
the face of a deadly hail of grape-shot, were absolutely terrific ;
when they reached the top the Mexicans seemed to lose all thought
of further defence, pouring in bewildered masses out of the doors
and windows nearest the city, and tumbling like a torrent of water
down the steep rocks. The Lieutenant, who was in Chapultepec
at the time, said that one thousand and fifty bombs fell on the
fortress before the assault ; the main tower, the battlements and

stairways are still broken and shattered from their effects. "Here," said he, as we walked along the summit terrace, "fifty of ours lie buried ; and down yonder"—pointing to the foot of the hill—"so many that they were never counted." I was deeply moved by his calm, sad manner, as he talked thus of the defeat and slaughter of his countrymen. I felt like a participant in the injury, and almost wished that he had spoken of us with hate and reproach.

I do not believe, however, that Mexican enmity to the United States has been increased by the war, but rather the contrary. During all my stay in the country I never heard a bitter word said against us. The officers of our army seem to have made friends everywhere, and the war, by throwing the natives into direct contact with foreigners, has greatly abated their former prejudice against all not of Spanish blood. The departure of our troops was a cause of general lamentation among the tradesmen of Mexico and Vera Cruz. Nothing was more common to me than to hear Generals Scott and Taylor mentioned by the Mexicans in terms of entire respect and admiration. "If you should see General Taylor," said a very intelligent gentleman to me, "tell him that the Mexicans all honor him. He has never given up their houses to plunder ; he has helped their wounded and suffering ; he is as humane as he is brave, and they can never feel enmity towards him." It may be that this generous forgetfulness of injury argues a want of earnest patriotism, but it was therefore none the less grateful to me as an American.

We took leave of our kind guide and descended the hill. It was now after sunset ; we drove rapidly through the darkening cypresses and across a little meadow to the wall of Molino del Rey. A guard admitted us into the courtyard, on one side of which loomed the tall structure of the mill ; the other sides were flanked with low buildings, flat-roofed, with heavy parapets of stone along the outside. Crossing the yard, we passed through another gate to the open ground where the attack was made. This battle, as is now generally known, was a terrible mistake, costing the Americans eight hundred lives without any return for the sacrifice. The low parapets of the courtyard concealed a battery of cannon, and as our troops came down the bare, exposed face of the hill, rank after rank was mowed away by their deadly discharge. The mill was taken, it is true, but, being perfectly commanded by the guns of Chapultepec, it was an untenable position.

It was by this time so dark that we returned to the city by the route we came, instead of taking the other aqueduct and following the line of Gen. Worth's advance to the Garita of San Cosmé. Landing at Mr. Belden's residence, the Hotel de Bazar, we went into the Café adjoining, sat down by a marble table under the ever-blooming trees of the court-yard, and enjoyed a *chirimoya* ice —how delicious, may readily be imagined when I state that this fruit in its native state resembles nothing so much as a rich vanilla cream. The Café de Bazar is kept by M. Arago, a brother of the French astronomer and statesman, and strikingly like him in features. At night, the light Moorish corridors around his fountained court-yard are lighted with gay-colored lamps, and knots of writers, politicians or stray tourists are gathered there until ten o'clock, when Mexican law obliges the place to be closed.

Mr. Peyton and myself procured a pair of spirited mustangs and one morning rode out to the village of Guadalupe, three miles on the road to Tampico. It was a bright, hot day, and Iztaccihuatl flaunted its naked snows in the sun. The road was crowded with arrieros and rancheros, on their way to and from the city—suspicious characters, some of them, but we had left our purses at home and taken our pistols along. The shrine of the Virgin was closed at the time, but we saw the little chapel in which it was deposited and the flight of steps cut in the rock, which all devout Christians are expected to ascend on their knees. The principal church in the place is a large, imposing structure, but there is a smaller building entirely of blue and white glazed tiles, the effect of which is remarkably neat and unique. Half way up the hill, some rich Mexican who was saved from shipwreck by calling upon the Virgin of Guadalupe, has erected a votive offering in the shape of an immense mast and three sails, looking, at a distance, like part of an actual ship.

After a week in Mexico, I prepared to leave for Vera Cruz, to meet the British steamer of the 16th of February. The seats in the diligence had all been engaged for ten days previous, and I was obliged to take a place in the *pescante*, or driver's box, for which I paid $34. Again I rolled my sarape around my scanty luggage and donned the well-worn corduroy coat. I took leave of my kind friend Mr. Parrot, and lay down to pass my last night in the city of the Montezumas.

CHAPTER XIX.

THE BASE OF POPOCATAPETL.

WHEN we were called up by the mozo, at four o'clock, the air was dark, damp and chilly: not a star was to be seen. The travelers who gathered to take their chocolate in the dining-hall wore heavy cloaks or sarapes thrown over the shoulder and covering the mouth. Among them was my companion from Guanajuato, Don Antonio de Campos. I climbed to my seat in the *pescante*, above the driver and groom, and waited the order to start. At last the inside was packed, the luggage lashed on behind, and the harness examined by lanterns, to see that it was properly adjusted. "*Vamos!*" cried the driver; the rope was jerked from the leaders, and away we thundered down the silent streets, my head barely clearing the swinging lamps, stretched from corner to corner. We passed through the great plaza, now dim and deserted: the towers of the Cathedral were lost in mist. Crossing the canal, we drove through dark alleys to the barrier of the city, where an escort of lancers, in waiting among the gloomy court-yards, quietly took their places on either side of us.

A chill fog hung over all the valley. The air was benumbing, and I found two coats insufficient to preserve warmth. There are no gardens and fields of maguey on this side of the city, as on that

of Tacubaya. Here and there, a plantation of maize interrupts the
uniformity of the barren plains of grass. In many places, the
marshy soil bordering on Lake Tezcuco, is traversed by deep
ditches, which render it partially fit for cultivation. Leaving the
shores of Tezcuco, we turned southward, changed horses at the
little Peñon, (an isolated hill, between Lakes Chalco and Xochi-
milco) and drove on to Ayotla. This is the point where the
American army under Gen. Scott left the main road to Mexico,
turning around the Peñon Grande, south of the town, and taking
the opposite shore of Lake Chalco. It is a small, insignificant
village, but prettily situated beside the lake and at the foot of the
towering Peñon; a little further, a road branches off to Ameca
and the foot of Popocatapetl. Here we left the valley, and began
ascending the barren slopes of the mountain. Clumps of unsightly
cactus studded the rocky soil, which was cut into rough arroyos
by the annual rains.

Slowly toiling up the ascent, we changed horses at a large hacienda, built on one of the steps of the mountains, whence, looking
backward, the view of the valley was charming. The Peñon
stood in front; southward, towards Ameca and Tenango,
stretched a great plain, belted with green wheat-fields and dotted
with the white towers of villages. The waters of Chalco were at
our feet, and northward, through a gap in the hills, the broad
sheet of Lake Tezcuco flashed in the sun. But it was not till
we had climbed high among the pine forests and looked out from
under the eaves of the clouds, that I fully realized the grandeur of
this celebrated view. The vision seemed to embrace a world at
one glance. The Valley of Mexico, nearly one hundred miles in
extent, lay below, its mountain-walls buried in the clouds which
hung like a curtain above the immense picture. But through a

8*

rift in this canopy, a broad sheet of sunshine slowly wandered over
the valley, now glimmering on the lakes and brightening the
green of the fields and gardens, and now lighting up, with wonderful effect, the yellow sides of the ranges of hills. Had the morning been clear, the view would have been more extended, but I do
not think its broadest and brightest aspect could have surpassed
in effect, the mysterious half-light, half-gloom in which I saw it.

The clouds rolled around us as I gazed, and the cold wind blew
drearily among the pines. Our escort, now increased to twelve
lancers, shortened their ascent by taking the mule paths. They
looked rather picturesque, climbing in single file through the
forest; their long blue cloaks hanging on their horses' flanks and
their red pennons fluttering in the mist. The rugged defiles
through which our road lay, are the most famous resort for robbers
in all Mexico. For miles we passed through one continued
ambush, where frequent crosses among the rocks hinted dark
stories of assault and death. Our valorous lancers lagged behind,
wherever the rocks were highest and the pines most thickly set;
I should not have counted a single moment on their assistance,
had we been attacked. I think I enjoyed the wild scenery of the
pass more, from its perils. The ominous gloom of the day and
the sound of the wind as it swept the trailing clouds through the
woods of pine, heightened this feeling to something like a positive
enjoyment.

When we reached the inn of Rio Frio, a little below the summit of the pass, on its eastern side, our greatest danger was over.
Breakfast was on the table, and the eggs, rice, guisados and frijoles
speedily disappeared before our sharp-set appetites. Luckily for
our hunger, the diligence from Puebla had not arrived. The little
valley of Rio Frio is hedged in by high, piny peaks, somewhat

resembling the Catskills. Below it, another wild, dangerous pass of two or three miles opens upon the fertile and beautiful table-land of Puebla. The first object which strikes the eye on emerging from the woods, is the peak of Malinche, standing alone on the plain, about midway between the mountain ranges which terminate, on the Mexican side, in Popocatapetl, on the Vera Cruz side, in Orizaba. I looked into the sky, above the tree-tops, for the snows of Iztaccihuatl and Popocatapetl, but only a few white streaks on the side of the former volcano, could be seen. A violent snow-storm was raging along its summit, and upon Popocatapetl, which was entirely hidden from sight.

The table-land on which we entered, descends, with a barely perceptible slant, to Puebla—a distance of forty miles. Its surface, fenceless, and almost boundless to the eye, is covered with wheat and maize. Fine roads cross it; and the white walls of haciendas, half-buried in the foliage of their gardens, dot it, at intervals, to the feet of the distant mountains. The driver, an intelligent Mexican, pointed out to me the various points of interest, as we passed along. He professed to speak a little English, too, which he said he had picked up from passengers on the road; but as all his English amounted only to a choice vocabulary of oaths, it told badly for the character of his passengers.

All afternoon the clouds covered the summits of the volcanoes, and stretching like a roof across the table-land, rested on the broad shoulders of Malinche. As the sun descended, they lifted a little, and I could see the sides of Popocatapetl as far as the limit of the snow; but his head was still hooded. At last, through a break just above the pinnacle of his cone, the light poured in a full blaze, silvering the inner edges of the clouds with a sudden and splendid lustre. The snowy apex of the mountain, bathed in full radiance, seemed brighter than the sun itself—a spot of light so pure, so inconceivably dazzling, that though I could not withdraw my gaze, the eye could scarcely bear its excess. Then, as the clouds rolled together once more, the sun climbing through numerous rifts, made bars of light in the vapory atmosphere, reaching from the sides of Popocatapetl to their bases, many leagues away, on the plain. It was as if the mountain genii who built the volcano had just finished their work, leaving these, the airy gangways of their scaffolding, still planted around it, to attest its marvellous size and grandeur.

The most imposing view of Popocatapetl is from the side towards Puebla. It is not seen, as from the valley of Mexico, over the rims of intermediate mountains, but the cone widens downward with an unbroken outline, till it strikes the smooth tableland. On the right, but separated by a deep gap in the range, is the broad, irregular summit of Iztaccihuatl, gleaming with snow. The signification of the name is the "White Lady," given by the Aztecs on account of a fancied resemblance in its outline to the figure of a reclining female. The mountain of Malinche, opposite to the volcanoes, almost rivals them in majestic appearance. It rises from a base of thirty miles in breadth, to a height of about thirteen thousand feet. I gazed long upon its cloudy top and wooded waist, which the sun belted with a beam of gold, for on its opposite side, on the banks of a river which we crossed just before reaching Puebla, stands the ancient city of Tlascala. The name of the volcano, Malinche, is an Aztec corruption of Mariana, the Indian wife of Cortez. I could not look upon it without an ardent desire to stand on its sides, and with Bernal Diaz in hand, trace out the extent of the territory once possessed by his brave and magnanimous allies.

On the other hand, between me and the sunset, stood a still more interesting memorial of the Aztec power. There, in full view, its giant terraces clearly defined against the sky, the topmost one crowned with cypress, loomed the Pyramid of Cholula! The lines of this immense work are for the most part distinctly cut; on the eastern side, only, they are slightly interrupted by vegetation, and probably the spoliation of the structure. Although several miles distant, and rising from the level of the plain, without the advantage of natural elevation, the size of the pyramid astonished me. It seems an abrupt hill, equal in height and imposing form to the long range in front of it, or the dark hill of Tlaloc behind. Even with Popocatapetl for a back-ground, its effect does not diminish. The Spaniards, with all their waste of gold on heavy cathedrals and prison-like palaces, have never equaled this relic of the barbaric empire they overthrew.

I do not know whether the resemblance between the outline of this pyramid and that of the land of Mexico, from sea to sea, has been remarked. It is certainly no forced similitude. There is the foundation terrace of the Tierra Caliente; the steep ascent to the second broad terrace of the table-land; and again, the succeeding ascent to the lofty, narrow plateau dividing the waters of the continent. If we grant that the forms of the pyramid, the dome, the pillar and the arch, have their antitypes in Nature, it is no fanciful speculation to suppose that the Aztecs, with that breadth of imagination common to intelligent barbarism, made *their world* the model for their temples of worship and sacrifice.

Cholula vanished in the dusk, as we crossed the river of Tlascala and entered the shallow basin in which stands Puebla. The many towers of its churches and convents showed picturesquely in the twilight. The streets were filled with gay crowds returning from the Alameda. Motley maskers, on horseback and on foot, reminded us that this was the commencement of Carnival. The great plaza into which we drove was filled with stands of fruit-venders, before each of which flared a large torch raised upon a pole. The cathedral is in better style, and shows to greater advantage than that of Mexico. So we passed to the Hotel de Diligencias, where a good dinner, in readiness, delighted us more than the carnival or the cathedral.

After the final dish of frijoles had been dispatched, I made a short night-stroll through the city. The wind was blowing strong and cold from the mountains, whistling under the arches of the cortal and flaring the red torches that burned in the market-place. The fruit-sellers, nevertheless, kept at their posts, exchanging jokes occasionally with a masked figure in some nondescript costume. I found shelter from the wind, at last, in a grand old church, near the plaza. The interior was brilliantly lighted, and the floor covered by kneeling figures. There was nothing in the church itself, except its vastness and dimness, to interest me ; but the choral music I there heard was not to be described. A choir of boys, alternating with one of rich masculine voices, over-ran the full peal of the organ, and filled the aisle with delicious harmony. There was a single voice, which seemed to come out of the air, in the pauses of the choral, and send its clear, trumpet-tones directly to the heart. As long as the exercises continued, I stood by the door, completely chained by those divine sounds. The incense finally faded ; the tapers were put out one by one ; the worshippers arose, took another dip in the basin of holy water, and retired ; and I, too, went back to the hotel, and tried to keep warm under cover of a single sarape.

The manufactures of Puebla are becoming important to Mexico

—the more so, from the comparative liberality which is now exercised towards foreigners. A few years ago, I was informed, a stranger was liable to be insulted, if not assaulted, in the streets ; but, latterly, this prejudice is vanishing. The table-land around the city is probably one of the finest grain countries in the world. Under a proper administration of Government, Puebla might become the first manufacturing town in Mexico.

CHAPTER XX.

RISING before three o'clock is no pleasant thing, on the high table-land of Puebla, especially when one has to face the cold from the foretop of a diligence ; but I contrived to cheat the early travel of its annoyance, by looking backward to Popocatapetl, which rose cold and unclouded in the morning twilight. We sped over fertile plains, past the foot of Malinche, and met the sunrise at the town of Amozoque, another noted robber-hold. In the arroyos which cross the road at its eastern gate a fight took place between the advanced guard of the American army and a body of Mexican soldiers, on the march to the capital.

From Amozoque the plain ascends, with a scarcely perceptible rise, to the summit of the dividing ridge, beyond Perote. The clouds, which had gathered again by this time, hid from our view the mountain barriers of the table-land, to the east and west. The second post brought us to Acajete, whose white dome and towers we saw long before reaching it, projected brightly against the pines of a steep mountain behind. One is only allowed time at the posts to stretch his legs and light a cigar. The horses—or mules, as the case may be—are always in readiness, and woe to the

unlucky traveler who stands a hundred yards from the diligence
when the rope is drawn away from the ramping leaders.

The insular mountain of Acajete shelters a gang of robbers
among its ravines, and the road, bending to the left around its
base, is hedged with ambush of the most convenient kind. The
driver pointed out to me a spot in the thicket where one of the
gang was shot not long before. Half-way up the acclivity, a
thread of blue smoke rose through the trees, apparently from
some hut or camp on a little shelf at the foot of a precipice.
Further than this, we saw nothing which seemed to denote their
propinquity. The pass was cleared, the horses changed at El
Pinal—a large hacienda on the north side of the mountain—and
we dashed on till nearly noon, when the spires of Nopaluca appeared behind a distant hill—the welcome heralds of breakfast!

Beyond this point, where a trail branches off to Orizaba, the
character of the scenery is entirely changed. We saw no longer
the green wheat-plains and stately haciendas of Puebla. The
road passed over an immense llano, covered with short, brown
grass, and swept by a furious wind. To the north, occasional
peaks—barren, rocky and desolate in their appearance,—rose at
a short distance from our path. On the other hand, the llano
stretched away for many a league, forming a horizon to the eye
before it reached the foot of the mountains. The wind frequently
increased to such a pitch that all trace of the landscape was lost.
Columns of dust, rising side by side from the plain, mingled as
they whirled along, shrouding us as completely as a Newfoundland
fog. The sun was at times totally darkened. My eyes, which
were strongly blood-shotten, from too much gazing at the snows of
Popocatapetl, were severely affected by this hurricane. But there
is no evil without some accompanying good ; and the same wind

which nearly stifled me with dust, at last brushed away the clouds from the smooth, gradual outline of Cofre de Perote, and revealed the shining head of Orizaba.

Beyond La Venta de Soto, the road skirts a striking peak of rock, whose outline is nearly that of an exact pyramid, several thousand feet in height. The mozo called it Monte Pizarro. From its dark ravines the robbers frequently sally, to attack travelers on the plain. At some distance from the road, I noticed a mounted guard who followed us till relieved by another, planted at short intervals. As the sunset came on, we reached a savage volcanic region, where the only vegetation scattered over the ridgy beds of black lava, was the yucca and the bristly cactus. There were no inhabitants; some huts, here and there, stood in ruins; and the solitary guard, moving like a shadow over the lava hills, only added to the loneliness and increased the impression of danger. I have seen many wild and bleak spots, but none so absolutely Tartarean in its aspect. There was no softer transition of scene to break the feeling it occasioned, for the nightfall deepened as we advanced, leaving everything in dusky shadow, but the vast bulk of Cofre de Perote, which loomed between me and the southern stars. At last, lights glimmered ahead ; we passed down a street lined with miserable houses, across a narrow and dirty plaza, and into a cramped court-yard. The worst dinner we ate on the whole journey was being prepared in the most cheerless of rooms. This was Perote.

I went out to walk after dinner, but did not go far. The squalid look of the houses, and the villanous expression of the faces, seen by the light of a few starving lamps, offered nothing attractive, and the wind by this time was more piercing than ever. Perote bears a bad reputation in every respect: its situation is the bleakest in Mexico, and its people the most shameless in their depredations. The diligence is frequently robbed at the very gates of the town. We slept with another blanket on our beds, and found the addition of our sarapes still desirable. The mozo awoke us at half-past two, to coffee and chocolate in the cold. I climbed into the pescante and drew the canvas cover of the top around my shoulders. The driver—an American, who had been twenty years on the road—gave the word of starting, and let his eight mules have full rein. Five lancers accompanied us—two some distance in advance, one on each side and one bringing up the rear. The stars shone with a frosty lustre, looking larger and brighter in the thin air. We journeyed for two hours in a half darkness, which nevertheless permitted me to see that the country was worth little notice by daylight—a bleak region, ten thousand feet above the sea, and very sparsely inhabited.

About sunrise we reached the summit of the pass, and commenced descending through scattering pine woods. The declivity was at first gradual, but when we had passed the bevelled slope of the summit ridge, our road lay along the very brink of the mountains overlooking everything that lay between them and the Gulf of Mexico. Immediately north of the pass, the mountain chain turns eastward, running towards the Gulf in parallel ridges, on the summits of which we looked down. The beds of the valleys, wild, broken, and buried in a wilderness but little visited, were lost in the dense air, which filled them like a vapor. Beginning at the region of lava and stunted pine, the eye travels downward, from summit to summit of the ranges, catching, at intervals, glimpses of gardens, green fields of grain, orange orchards, groves of palm and gleaming towers, till at last it rests on the far-away glimmer of the sea, under the morning sun. Fancy yourself riding along

the ramparts of a fortress ten thousand feet in height, with all the
climates of the earth spread out below you, zone lying beyond zone,
and the whole bounded at the furthest horizon to which vision can
reach, by the illimitable sea! Such is the view which meets one
on descending to Jalapa.

The road was broad and smooth, and our mules whirled us
downward on a rapid gallop. In half an hour from the time when
around us the hoar-frost was lying on black ridges of lava and
whitening the tips of the pine branches, we saw the orange and
banana, basking in the glow of a region where frost was
unknown. We were now on the borders of paradise. The
streams, leaping down crystal-clear from the snows of Cofre de
Perote, fretted their way through tangles of roses and blossoming
vines; the turf had a sheen like that of a new-cut emerald; the
mould, upturned for garden land, showed a velvety richness and
softness, and the palm, that true child of light, lifted its slender
shaft and spread its majestic leaves against the serene blue of
heaven. As we came out of the deep-sunken valleys on the brow
of a ridge facing the south, there stood, distinct and shadowless
from base to apex, the Mountain of Orizaba. It rose beyond
mountains so far off that all trace of chasm or ledge or belting
forest was folded in a veil of blue air, yet its grand, immaculate
cone, of perfect outline, was so white, so dazzling, so pure in its
frozen clearness, like that of an Arctic morn, that the eye lost its
sense of the airy gulf between, and it seemed that I might stretch
out my hand and touch it. No peak among mountains can be
more sublime than Orizaba. Rising from the level of the sea and
the perpetual summer of the tropics, with an unbroken line to the
height of eighteen thousand feet, it stands singly above the other
ranges with its spotless crown of snow, as some giant, white-haired

Northern king might stand among a host of the weak, effeminate sybarites of the South. Orizaba dwells alone in my memory, as the only perfect type of a mountain to be found on the Earth.

After two leagues of this enchanting travel we came to Jalapa, a city of about twenty thousand inhabitants, on the slope of the hills, half-way between the sea and the table-land, overlooking the one and dominated by the other. The streets are as clean as a Dutch cottage; the one-story, tiled houses, sparkling in the sun, are buried in gardens that rival the Hesperides. Two miles before reaching the town the odor of its orange blossoms filled the air. We descended its streets to the Diligence Hotel, at the bottom, where, on arriving, we found there would be no stage to Vera Cruz for two days, so we gave ourselves up to the full enjoyment of the spot. My fellow-passenger for Guanajuato, Don Antonio de Campos, and myself, climbed into the tower of the hotel, and sat down under its roof to enjoy the look-out. The whole landscape was like a garden. For leagues around the town it was one constant alternation of field, grove and garden—the fields of the freshest green, the groves white with blossoms and ringing with the songs of birds, and the gardens loading the air with delicious perfume. Stately haciendas were perched on the vernal slopes, and in the fields; on the roads and winding mule-paths of the hills we saw everywhere a gay and light-hearted people. We passed the whole afternoon in the tower; the time went by like a single pulsation of delight. I felt, then, that there could be no greater happiness than in thus living forever, without a single thought beyond the enjoyment of the scene. My friend, Don Antonio, was busy with old memories. Twenty years before, he came through Jalapa for the first time, an ardent, aspiring youth, thinking to achieve his fortune in three or four years and return with it to his native

Portugal; but alas! twenty years had barely sufficed for the fulfilment of his dreams—twenty years of toil among the barren
mountains of Guanajuato. Now, he said, all that time vanished
from his mind; his boyish glimpse of Jalapa was his Yesterday,
and the half-forgotten life of his early home lay close behind it.

After dinner, all our fellow-travelers set out for the Alameda,
which lies in a little valley at the foot of the town. A broad
paved walk, with benches of stone at the side and stone urns on
lofty pedestals at short intervals, leads to a bridge over a deep
chasm, where the little river plunges through a mesh of vines into
a large basin below. Beyond this bridge, a dozen foot-paths lead
off to the groves and shaded glens, the haciendas and orange
orchards. The idlers of the town strolled back and forth, enjoying
the long twilight and balmy air. We were all in the most joyous
mood, and my fellow-passengers of three or four different nations
expressed their delight in as many tongues, with an amusing
contrast of exclamations: " *Ah, que joli petit pays de Jalape !*"
cried the little Frenchwoman, who had talked in a steady stream
since leaving Mexico, notwithstanding she was going to France on
account of delicate lungs. " *Siente usté el aroma de las naran-
jas ?*" asked a dark-eyed Andalusian. " *Himmlische Luft !*"
exclaimed the enraptured German, unconsciously quoting Götz
von Berlichingen. Don Antonio turned to me, saying in
English: " My pulse is quicker and my blood warmer than for
twenty years; I believe my youth is actually coming back again."
We talked thus till the stars came out and the perfumed air was cool
with invisible dew.

When we awoke the next morning it was raining, and continued
to rain all day—not a slow, dreary drizzle, nor a torrent of heavy
drops, as rain comes to us, but a fine, ethereal, gauzy veil of mois-

ture that scarcely stirred the grass on which it fell or shook the light golden pollen from the orange flowers. Every two or three days such a shower comes down on the soil of Jalapa—

" a perpetual April to the ground,
Making it all one emerald."

We could not stroll among the gardens or sit under the urns of the Alameda, but the towers and balconies were left us ; the landscape, though faint and blurred by the filmy rain, was nearly as beautiful, and the perfume could not be washed out of the air. So passed the day, and with the night we betook ourselves early to rest, for the Diligence was to leave at three o'clock on the morrow.

For two leagues after leaving Jalapa I smelt the orange blossoms in the starry morning, but when daylight glimmered on the distant Gulf, we were riding between bleak hills, covered with chapparal, having descended to the barren heats of the tropical winter, beyond the line of the mountain-gathered showers. The road was rough and toilsome, but our driver, an intelligent American, knew every stone and rut in the dark and managed his eight mules with an address and calculation which seemed to me marvellous. He had been on the road six years, at a salary of $150 per month, from the savings of which he had purchased a handsome little property in Jalapa. Don Juan, as the natives called him, was a great favorite along the road, which his sturdy, upright character well deserved. At sunrise we reached the hacienda of El Encero, belonging to Santa Anna, as do most of the other haciendas between Jalapa and Vera Cruz. The hill of Cerro Gordo appeared before us, and a drive of an hour brought us to the cluster of cane-huts bearing the same name.

The physical features of the field of Cerro Gordo are very interesting. It is a double peak, rising from the midst of rough, rolling hills, covered with a dense thicket of cactus and thorny shrubs. Towards Vera Cruz it is protected by deep barrancas and passes, which in proper hands might be made impregnable. Had Gen. Scott attempted to take it by advancing up the broad highway, he must inevitably have lost the battle ; but by cutting a road through the chapparal with great labor, making a circuit of several miles, he reached the north-eastern slope of the hill—the most accessible point, and according to the Mexican story, the side least defended. Having gained one of the peaks of the hill, the charge was made down the side and up the opposite steep in the face of the Mexican batteries. The steady march of our forces under this deadly hail, to the inspiring blast of the Northern bugles, has been described to me by officers who took part in the fight, as the most magnificent spectacle of the war. After taking the battery, the guns were turned upon the Mexicans, who were flying through the chapparal in all directions. Many, overcome by terror, leaped from the brink of the barranca at the foot of the hill and were crushed to death in the fall. Santa Anna, who escaped at this place, was taken down by a path known to some of the officers. The chapparal is still strewn thickly with bleached bones, principally of the mules and horses who were attached to the ammunition wagons of the enemy. The driver told me that until recently there were plenty of cannon-balls lying beside the road, but that every American, English or French traveler took one as a relic, till there were no more to be seen. A shallow cave beside the road was pointed out as the spot where the Mexicans hid their ammunition. It was not discovered by our troops, but a Mexican who knew the secret, sold it to them out of re-

venge for the non-payment of some mules which he had furnished
to his own army.   The driver lay hidden in Jalapa for some days
previous to the battle, unable to escape, and the first intelligence
he received of what had taken place, was that furnished by the
sight of the flying Mexicans.   They poured through the town that
evening and the day following, he said, in the wildest disorder,
some mounted on donkeys, some on mules, some on foot, many of
the officers without hats or swords, others wrapped in the dusty
coat of a private, and all cursing, gesticulating and actually weep-
ing, like men crazed.   They had been so confident of success that
the reverse seemed almost heart-breaking.

A few miles beyond Cerro Gordo we reached Plan del Rio, a
small village of cane huts, which was burned down by order of
Santa Anna, on the approach of the American forces.   A splendid stone bridge across the river was afterwards blown up by the
guerillas, in the foolish idea that they would stop an American
specie-train, coming from Vera Cruz.   In half a day after the
train arrived there was an excellent road across the chasm, and
the Mexicans use it to this day, for the shattered arch has never
been rebuilt.   From Plan del Rio to the Puente Nacional is about
three leagues, through the same waste of cactus and chapparal.
The latter place, the scene of many a brush with the guerillas
during the war, is in a very wild and picturesque glen, through
which the river forces its way to the sea.   The bridge is one of
the most magnificent structures of the kind on the continent.   On
a little knoll, at the end towards Jalapa, stands a stately hacienda
belonging to Santa Anna.

We sped on through the dreary chapparal, now sprinkled with
palms and blossoming trees.   The country is naturally rich and
productive, but is little better than a desert.   The only inhabitants

are a set of half-naked Indians, who live in miserable huts, supporting themselves by a scanty cultivation of maize, and the deer they kill in the thickets. Just before we reached the sea-shore, one of these people came out of the woods, with a little spotted fawn in his arms, which he offered to sell. The driver bought it for a dollar, and the beautiful little creature, not more than two weeks old, was given to me to carry. I shielded it from the cold sea-wind, and with a contented bleat it nestled down in my lap and soon fell fast asleep.

At sunset we drove out on the broad sands bordering the Gulf. A chill norther was blowing, and the waves thundered over the coral reefs with a wintry sound. Vera Cruz sat on the bleak shore, a league before us, her domes and spires painted on the gloomy sky. The white walls of San Juan d'Ulloa rose from the water beyond the shipping. Not a tree or green thing was to be seen for miles around the city, which looked as completely desolate as if built in the middle of Zahara. Nevertheless, I blessed the sight of it, and felt a degree of joy as I passed within its gates, for the long journey of twelve hundred miles across the Continent was safely accomplished

CHAPTER XXI.

I CANNOT say much of Vera Cruz. A town built and sustained by commerce alone, and that not the most flourishing, presents few points of interest to the traveler. Its physiognomy differs but little from that of the other Mexican cities I have described. There is the Plaza, flanked by the Cathedral,—the same pink mass of old Spanish architecture, picturesque only for its associations—the Diligence Hotel, with its arched corridor forming a *cortal* along one side—the dreary, half-deserted streets, with their occasional palaces of stone enclosing paved and fountained courtyards—the market, heaped with the same pyramids of fruit which have become so familiar to us—the dirty adobe huts, nearest the walls, with their cut-throat population—and finally, the population itself, rendered more active, intelligent and civilized by the presence of a large number of foreigners, but still comprised mainly of the half-breed, with the same habits and propensities as we find in the interior. The town is contracted ; standing in the plaza, one can see its four corners, bounded by the walls and the sea, and all within a few minutes' walk. Outside of the gates we come at once upon the deserts of sand.

On reaching Vera Cruz, there were no tidings of the steamer, which was due on the 4th. The U. S. schooner Flirt, Capt. Farren, was in port waiting for a norther to go down, to sail for New Orleans, but there was small chance of passage on board of her. On the morning of the 15th, the U. S. steamer Water-witch, Capt. Totten, made her appearance, bound homeward after a cruise to Havana, Sisal, Campeachy and Laguna. I had almost determined, in default of any other opportunity, to take passage in her, as a "distressed citizen," when, on rowing out to the Castle of San Juan d'Ulloa on the third morning, one of the boat-men descried a faint thread of smoke on the horizon. "*El vapor!*" was the general exclamation, and at least fifty dissatisfied persons recovered their good-humor.

My friend Don Antonio was acquainted with the Commandante of the Castle, Don Manuel Robles, by which means we obtained free admission within its coral walls. It is a place of immense strength, and in the hands of men who know how to defend it, need no more be taken than Gibraltar. We climbed to the top of the tower, walked around the parapets, shouted into the echoing wells sunk deep in the rock, and examined its gigantic walls. The spongy coral of which it is built receives the shot and shells that have been thrown upon it, without splintering; here and there we noticed holes where they had imbedded themselves in it, rather adding to its solidity. We sat two or three hours in the tower, watching the approaching smoke of the steamer. As the chimes rang noon in Vera Cruz, a terrific blast of trumpets pealed through the courtyard of the Castle, below us. The yellow-faced soldiers, in their white shirts and straw hats with the word "Ulua" upon them, mustered along one side, and after a brief drill, had their dinner of rice, frijoles and coffee served to them. The force in the Castle appeared very small ; the men were buried in its immense vaults and galleries, and at times, looking down from the tower, scarcely a soul was to be seen.   The Commandante invited us to his quarters, and offered us refreshments, after we had made the round of the parapets.   Singularly enough, his room was hung with American engravings of the battles of the late war

The most interesting object in Vera Cruz is an old church, in the southern part of the city, which was built by Cortez, in 1531 —the oldest Christian church in the New World. Some miles distant is the old town of Vera Cruz, which was abandoned for the present site. I had not time to visit it, nor the traces of the Americans among the sand-hills encircling the city.   One Sunday evening, however, I visited the *paseo*, a paved walk outside the gate, with walls to keep off the sand and some miserable attempts at trees here and there. As it was Carnival, the place was crowded, but most of the promenaders appeared to be foreigners. Beyond the paseo, however, stood a cluster of half-ruined buildings, where the lower class of the native population was gathered at a fandango.   After the arrival of the steamer nothing was talked of but our departure and nothing done but to pack trunks and contrive ways of smuggling money, in order to avoid the export duty of six per cent.

We left Vera Cruz on the morning of February 19th, and reached Tampico Bar after a run of twenty-two hours.   The surf was so high after the recent norther, that we were obliged to wait three days before the little river-steamer could come to us with her million of dollars. The Thames, however, was so spacious and pleasant a ship, that we were hardly annoyed by the delay.   Coming from semi-civilized Mexico, the sight of English order and the en-

joyment of English comfort were doubly agreeable. Among our
passengers were Lady Emeline Stuart Wortley, returning from a
heroic trip to Mexico ; Lord Mark Kerr, a gentleman of intelligence and refinement, and an amateur artist of much talent; and
Mr. Hill, an English traveler, on his way home after three years
spent in Russia, Siberia, Polynesia, and the interior of South
America.   My eight days spent on board the Thames, passed
away rapidly, and on the afternoon of the 26th, we made the
light-house on Mobile Point, and came-to among the shipping at
the anchorage.   I transferred myself and sarape to the deck of a
high-pressure freight-boat, and after lying all night in the bay, on
account of a heavy fog, set foot next morning on the wharf at
Mobile.

Leaving the same afternoon, I passed two days on the beautiful
Alabama River ; was whirled in the cars from Montgomery to
Opelika, and jolted twenty-four hours in a shabby stage, over the
hills of Georgia, to the station of Griffin, on the Central Railroad ;
sped away through Atlanta and Augusta to Charleston ; tossed a
night on the Atlantic, crossed the pine-barrens of Carolina and
the impoverished fields of the Old Dominion ; halted a day at
Washington to deliver dispatches from Mexico, a day at HOME, in
Pennsylvania, and finally reached my old working-desk in the Tri-
bune Office on the night of March 10th—just eight months and
eight days from the time of my departure.

Thus closed a journey more novel and adventurous than any I
hope to make again.   I trust the profit of it has not been wholly
mine, but that the reader who has followed me through the fore-
going pages, may find some things in them, which to have read
were not also to have forgotten.

APPENDIX.

APPENDIX.

REPORT OF HON. T. BUTLER KING.

Washington, March 22, 1850.

Sir: In obedience to your instructions, dated the 3d of April last, I proceeded to California by way of the Isthmus of Panama, and arrived at San Francisco on the 4th day of June.

The steamer in which I took passage was the first conveyance that reached California with intelligence of the inauguration of President Taylor and the appointment of his Cabinet, and that Congress had failed to aid the Executive in providing a government for the people of that Territory. The greatest anxiety was naturally felt and manifested to ascertain the cause of this neglect on the part of the Government of the United States, and what steps duty to themselves required them to take, in the painful and embarrassing position in which they were placed, for their protection and welfare.

A brief sketch of their condition will explain the cause of this anxiety.

The discovery of the gold mines had attracted a very large number of citizens of the United States to that Territory, who had never been accustomed to any other than American law, administered by American courts. There they found their rights of property and person subject to the uncertain, and frequently most oppressive, operation of laws written in a language they did not understand, and founded on principles, in many respects, new to them. They complained that the alcaldes, or judges, most of whom had been appointed or elected before the immigration had commenced, were not lawyers by education or profession; and, being Americans, they were, of course, unacquainted with the laws of Mexico, or the principles of the civil law on which they are founded.

As our own laws, except for the collection of Revenue, the transmission of the mails, and establishment of post offices, had not been extended over that Territory, the laws of Mexico, as they existed at the conclusion of the treaty of Guadalupe Hidalgo, regulating the relations of the inhabitants of California with each other, necessarily remained in force;* yet, there was not a single volume containing those laws, as far as I know or believe, in the whole Territory, except, perhaps, in the Governor's office, at Monterey.

The magistrates, therefore, could not procure them, and the administration of justice was, necessarily, as unequal and fluctuating as the opinions of the judges were conflicting and variable.

There were no fee bills to regulate costs, and, consequently, the most cruel exactions, in many instances, were practised.

The greatest confusion prevailed respecting titles to property, and the decision of suits, involving the most important rights, and very large sums of money depended upon the dictum of the judge.

The sale of the Territory by Mexico to the United States had necessarily cut off or dissolved the laws regulating the granting or procuring titles to land; and, as our own land laws had not been extended over it, the people were compelled to receive such titles as were offered to them, without the means of ascertaining whether they were valid or not.

Litigation was so expensive and precarious, that injustice and oppression were frequently endured, rather than resort to so uncertain a remedy.

Towns and cities were springing into existence—many of them without charters or any legal right to organize municipal authorities, or to tax property or the citizens for the establishment of a police, the erection of prisons, or providing any of those means for the protection of life and property which are so necessary in all civil communities, and especially among a people mostly strangers to each other.

* See American Insurance Company et al. vs. Canter. 1st Peters's Supreme Court Reports, 542.

Nearly one million and a half of dollars had been paid into the Custom Houses, as duties on imported goods, before our revenue laws had been extended over the country ; and the people complained bitterly that they were thus heavily taxed without being provided with a Government for their protection, or laws which they could understand, or allowed the right to be represented in the councils of the nation.

While anxiously waiting the action of Congress, oppressed and embarrassed by this state of affairs and feeling the pressing necessity of applying such remedies as were in their power and circumstances seemed to justify, they resolved to substitute laws of their own for the existing system, and to establish tribunals for their proper and faithful administration.

In obedience, therefore, to the extraordinary exigencies of their condition, the people of the city of San Francisco elected members to form a legislature, and clothed them with full powers to pass laws.

The communities of Sonoma and of Sacramento City followed the example.

Thus were three legislative bodies organized ; the two most distant being only one hundred and thirty miles apart.

Other movements of the kind were threatened, and doubtless would have been followed in other sections of the Territory, had they not been arrested by the formation of a State Government.

While the people of California were looking to Congress for a Territorial Government, it was quite evident that such an organization was daily becoming less suited to their condition, which was entirely different from that of any of the Territories out of which the new States of the Union had been formed.

Those Territories had been at first slowly and sparsely peopled by a few hunters and farmers, who penetrated the wilderness, or traversed the prairies in search of game or a new home ; and, when thus gradually their population warranted it, a government was provided for them. They, however, had no foreign commerce, nor anything beyond the ordinary pursuits of agriculture and the various branches of business which usually accompany it, to induce immigration within their borders. Several years were required to give them sufficient population and wealth to place them in a condition to require, or enable them to support, a State Government.

Not so with California. The discovery of the vast metallic and mineral wealth in her mountains had already attracted to her, in the space of twelve months, more than one hundred thousand people; an extensive commerce had sprung up with China, the ports of Mexico on the Pacific, Chili, and Australia.

Hundreds of vessels from the Atlantic ports of the Union, freighted with our manufactures and agricultural products, and filled with our fellow citizens, had arrived, or were on their passage round Cape Horn; so that in the month of June last there were more than three hundred sea-going vessels in the port of San Francisco.

California has a border on the Pacific of ten degrees of latitude, and several important harbors which have never been surveyed; nor is there a buoy, a beacon, a light-house, or a fortification, on the whole coast.

There are no docks for the repair of national or mercantile vessels nearer than New York, a distance of some twenty thousand miles round Cape Horn.

All these things, together with the proper regulations of the gold region, the quicksilver mines, the survey and disposition of the public lands, the adjustment of land titles, the establishment of a mint and of marine hospitals, required the immediate formation of a more perfect Civil Government than California then had, and the fostering care of Congress and the Executive.

California had, as it were by magic, become a State of great wealth and power. One short year had given her a commercial importance but little inferior to that of the most powerful of the old States. She had passed her minority at a single bound, and might justly be regarded as fully entitled to take her place as an equal among her sisters of the Union.

When, therefore, the reality became known to the people of that Territory that the government had done nothing to relieve them from the evils and embarrassments under which they were suffering, and seeing no probability of any change on the subject which divided Congress, they adopted, with most unexampled unanimity and promptitude, the only course which lay open to them—the immediate formation of a State Government.

They were induced to take this step not only for the reason that it promised the most speedy remedy for present difficulties, but because the great and rapidly growing interests of the Territory demanded it; and all reflecting men saw, at a glance, that it ought not to be any longer, and could not under any circumstances, be much longer postponed.

They not only considered themselves best qualified, but that they had the right to decide, as far as they were concerned, the embarrassing question which was shaking the Union to its centre, and had thus far deprived them of a regularly organized civil government. They believed that, in forming a constitution they had a right to establish or prohibit slavery, and that in their action as a State, they would be sustained by the North and the South.

They were not unmindful of the fact, that while Northern statesmen had contended that Congress has power to prohibit slavery in the Territories they had always admitted that the States of the Union had the right to abolish or establish it at pleasure.

On the other hand, Southern statesmen had almost unanimously contended that Congress has not the constitutional power to *prohibit* slavery in the Territories, because they have not the power to *establish* it; but that the people, in forming a government for themselves, have the right to do either. If Congress can rightfully do one, they can certainly do the other.

This is the doctrine put forth by Mr. Calhoun in his celebrated resolutions of 1847, introduced into the Senate of the United States, among which is the following:

"*Resolved*, That it is a fundamental principle in our political creed, that a people in forming a constitution have the unconditional right to form and adopt the government which they may think best calculated to secure their liberty, prosperity and happiness; and, in conformity thereto, no other condition is imposed by the Federal Constitution on a State, in order to be admitted into this Union, except that its constitution shall be 'Republican;' and that the imposition of any other by Congress would not only be in violation of the Constitution, but in direct conflict with the principle on which our political system rests."

President Polk, in his annual message, dated 5th December, 1848, uses the following language:

"The question is believed to be rather abstract than practical, whether slavery ever can or would exist in any portion of the acquired territory, even if it were left to the option of the slaveholding States themselves. From the nature of the climate and productions, in much the larger portion of it, it is certain it could never exist; and in the remainder the probabilities are that it would not.

"But, however this may be, the question, involving, as it does, a principle of equality of rights of the separate and several States, as equal copartners in the confederacy, should not be disregarded.

"In organizing governments over these Territories, no duty imposed on Congress by the Constitution requires that they should legislate on the subject of slavery, while their power to do so is not only seriously questioned, but denied, by many of the soundest expounders of that instrument.

"Whether Congress shall legislate or not, the people of the acquired Territories, when assembled in Convention to form State Constitutions, will possess the sole and exclusive power to determine for themselves whether slavery shall or shall not exist within their limits."

The people of California, therefore, acting in conformity with the views thus expressed, and what seemed to be the generally admitted opinion in the States, had every reason to suppose, and did suppose, that by forming a Constitution for themselves, and deciding this question in accordance with their own views and interests, they would be received with open arms by all parties.

In taking this step they proceeded with all the regularity which has ever characterized the American people in discharging the great and important duties of self-government.

As already stated, I arrived at San Francisco on the morning of the 4th of June.

The steamer in which I was a passenger did not stop at Monterey; I therefore did not see General Riley, nor had I any communication with him until about the middle of the month, when he came to San Francisco. A few days after my arrival his proclamation calling a Convention to form a State Constitution, *dated the third of June*, was received.

The people acted in compliance with what they believed to be the views of Congress, and conformably to the recommendations of the proclamation, and proceeded, on the day appointed, to elect members to a Convention for the purpose of forming a constitution, to be regularly submitted to the people for their ratification or rejection, and, if approved, to be presented to Congress, with a prayer for the admission of California, as a State, into the Union.

I desire here to make a brief and emphatic reply to the various unjust and most extraordinary accusations and insinuations which have been made respecting the movements of the people of California in forming their State Government.

I had no secret instructions, verbal or written, from the President, or any one else, what to say to the people of California on the subject of slavery; nor was it ever hinted or intimated to me that I was expected to attempt to influence their action in the slightest degree on that subject. That I never did, the people of California will bear me witness. In that Territory there was none of the machinery of party or of the press; and it is even more absurd to suppose that any *secret influences*, for or against slavery, could have been used there, than it would to believe that they could be successfully employed in Maryland or Georgia.

I therefore declare all assertions and insinuations, that I was secretly instructed to, or that I did in any way, attempt to influence the people of California to exclude slavery from their Territory, to be without foundation.

The election of delegates to the Convention proceeded regularly in pursuance of the proposed mode of holding it, and as far as I am informed, no questions were asked whether a candidate was a Whig or a Democrat, or whether he was from the North or the South. The only object seemed to be, to find competent men who were willing to make the sacrifice of time which a proper discharge of their duties would require.

As soon after my arrival at San Francisco as the arrangements of General Smith would permit, I proceeded with him to the interior of the country for the purpose of examining the gold region, and other interesting and important portions of it. I did not return until the 16th of August. The elections had taken place when I was in the mountains. I was taken ill on the 20th of that month, and was confined to my bed and room more than two months.

The Convention met on the 1st of September. So it will be seen that I was not present where any election was held, nor had I anything to do with selecting or bringing out candidates; and my illness is sufficient proof that I did not, and could not, had I been disposed, exercise any influence in the Convention, which was sitting one hundred and thirty miles from where I was.

Some intimations or assertions, as I am informed, have been thrown out that the South was not fairly represented in the Convention. I am told by two of the members of Congress elect from California, who were members of the Convention, that of the thirty-seven delegates designated in General Riley's proclamation, sixteen were from slaveholding, ten from the non-slaveholding States, and eleven who were citizens of California under the Mexican government, and that ten of those eleven came from districts below 36° 30'. So that there were in the Convention twenty-six of the thirty-seven members from the slaveholding States and from places south of the Missouri Compromise line.

It appears, on the journals of the Convention, that the clause in the constitution excluding slavery passed unanimously.

I now proceed to give the result of my inquiries, observations and reflections respecting the population, climate, soil, productions—the general character of grants of land from Mexico—the extent and condition of the public domain—the commercial resources and prospects—the mineral and metallic wealth of California.

POPULATION.

Humboldt, in his Essay on New Spain, states the population of Upper California, in 1802, to have consisted of—

Converted Indians	15,562
Other Classes	1,300
Total	16,862

Alexander Forbes, in his history of Upper and Lower California, published in London
in 1839, states the number of converted Indians in the former to have been,

In 1831..18,683

   Of all other Classes, at... 4,342

         Total... 23,025

He expresses the opinion that the number had not varied much up to
1835, and the probability is, there was very little increase in the white
population until the emigrants from the United States began to enter the
country in 1838.

They increased, from year to year, so that, in 1846, Col. Fremont had
little difficulty in calling to his standard some five hundred fighting men.

At the close of the war with Mexico it was supposed that there were,
including discharged volunteers, from ten to fifteen thousand Americans
and Californians, exclusive of converted Indians, in the Territory. The
immigration of American citizens in 1849, up to the 1st January last, was
estimated at eighty thousand—of foreigners, twenty thousand.

The population of California may therefore be safely set down at
115,000 at the commencement of the present year.

It is quite impossible to form anything like an accurate estimate of the
number of Indians in the Territory. Since the commencement of the
war, and especially since the discovery of gold in the mountains, their
numbers at the missions and in the valleys near the coast have very much
diminished. In fact the whole race seems to be rapidly disappearing.

The remains of a vast number of villages in all the valleys of the Sierra
Nevada, and among the foot-hills of that range of mountains, show that
at no distant day there must have been a numerous population where
there is not now an Indian to be seen. There are a few still retained in
the service of the old Californians, but these do not amount to more than
a few thousand in the whole Territory. It is said there are large numbers of them in the mountains and valleys about the head waters of the
San Joaquin, along the western base of the Sierra, and in the northern
part of the Territory, and that they are hostile. A number of Americans were killed by them during the last summer in attempting to pene-
trate high up the rivers in search of gold ; they also drove one or two
parties from Trinity River. They have in several instances attacked

parties coming from or returning to Oregon, in the section of country which the lamented Captain Warner was examining when he was killed.

It is quite impossible to form any estimate of the number of these mountain Indians. Some suppose there are as many as 300,000 in the Territory, but I should not be inclined to believe that there can be one third of that number. It is quite evident that they are hostile, and that they ought to be chastised for the murders already committed.

The small bands with whom I met, scattered through the lower portions of the foot-hills of the Sierra, and the valleys between them and the coast, seemed to be almost of the lowest grade of human beings. They live chiefly on acorns, roots, insects, and the kernel of the pine burr—occasionally they catch fish and game. They use the bow and arrow, but are said to be too lazy and effeminate to make successful hunters. They do not appear to have the slightest inclination to cultivate the soil, nor do they even attempt it—as far as I could obtain information—except when they are induced to enter the service of the white inhabitants. They have never pretended to hold any interest in the soil, nor have they been treated by the Spanish or American immigrants as possessing any.

The Mexican government never treated with them for the purchase of land, or the relinquishment of any claim of it whatever. They are lazy, idle to the last degree, and, although they are said to be willing to give their services to any one who will provide them with blankets, beef and bread, it is with much difficulty they can be made to perform labor enough to reward their employers for these very limited means of comfort.

Formerly, at the missions, those who were brought up and instructed by the priests, made very good servants. Many of those now attached to families seem to be faithful and intelligent. But those who are at all in a wild and uncultivated state are most degraded objects of filth and idleness.

It is possible that government might, by collecting them together, teach them, in some degree, the arts and habits of civilization; but, if we may judge of the future from the past, they will disappear from the face of the earth as the settlements of the whites extend over the country. A very considerable military force will be necessary, however, to protect the emigrants in the northern and southern portions of the Territory

CLIMATE.

I now come to consider the climate. The climate of California is so remarkable in its periodical changes, and for the long continuance of the wet and dry seasons, dividing, as they do, the year into about two equal parts, which have a most peculiar influence on the labor applied to agriculture and the products of the soil, and, in fact, connect themselves so inseparably with all the interests of the country, that I deem it proper briefly to mention the causes which produce these changes, and which, it will be seen, as this report proceeds, must exercise a controlling influence on the commercial prosperity and resources of the country.

It is a well-established theory, that the currents of air under which the earth passes in its diurnal revolutions follow the line of the sun's greatest attraction. These currents of air are drawn toward this line from great distances on each side of it; and as the earth revolves from west to east, they blow from northeast and southeast, meeting, and of course causing a calm, on the line.

Thus, when the sun is directly, in common parlance, over the equator, in the month of March, these currents of air blow from some distance north of the tropic of Cancer, and south of the tropic of Capricorn, in an oblique direction toward this line of the sun's greatest attraction, and forming what are known as the northeast and southeast trade winds.

As the earth, in its path round the sun, gradually brings the *line* of attraction north, in summer these currents of air are carried *with* it; so that about the middle of May the current from the northeast has extended as far as the 38th or 39th degree of north latitude, and by the 20th of June, the period of the sun's greatest northern inclination, to the northern portions of California and the southern section of Oregon.

These northeast winds, in their progress across the continent, toward the Pacific Ocean, pass over the snow-capped ridges of the Rocky Mountains and the Sierra Nevada, and are of course deprived of all the moisture which can be extracted from them by the low temperature of those regions of eternal snow, and consequently no moisture can be precipitated from them, in the form of dew or rain, in a higher temperature than that to which they have been subjected. They therefore pass over the hills and plains of California, where the temperature is very high in summer, in a very dry state; and so far from being charged with moisture, they absorb, like a sponge, all that the atmosphere and surface of the earth can yield, until both become, apparently, perfectly dry.

This process commences, as I have said, when the line of the sun's greatest attraction comes north in summer, bringing with it these vast atmospheric movements, and on their approach produce the dry season in California, which, governed by these laws, continues until some time after the sun repasses the equator in September, when, about the middle of November, the climate being relieved from these northeast currents of air, the southwest winds set in from the ocean, charged with moisture—the rains commence and continue to fall not constantly, as some persons have represented, but with sufficient frequency to designate the period of their continuance, from about the middle of November until the middle of May, in the latitude of San Francisco, as the wet season.

It follows as a matter of course, that the *dry season* commences first, and continues longest in the southern portions of the Territory, and that the climate of the northern part is influenced in a much less degree, by the causes which I have mentioned, than any other section of the country. Consequently, we find that as low down as latitude 39°, rains are sufficiently frequent in summer to render irrigation quite unnecessary to the perfect maturity of any crop which is suited to the soil and climate.

There is an extensive ocean current of cold water, which comes from the northern regions of the Pacific, or, perhaps from the Arctic, and flows along the coast of California. It comes charged with, and emits in its progress, air, which appears in the form of fog when it comes in contact with a higher temperature on the American coast, as the Gulf stream of the Atlantic exhales vapor when it meets in any part of its progress, a lower temperature. This current has not been surveyed, and, therefore, its source, temperature, velocity, width and course have not been accurately ascertained.

It is believed by Lieutenant Maury, on what he considers sufficient evidence—and no higher authority can be cited—that the current comes from the coasts of China and Japan, flows northwardly to the peninsula of Kamtschatka, and, making a circuit to the eastward, strikes the American coast in about latitude 41° or 42°. It passes thence southwardly, and finally loses itself in the tropics.

Below latitude 39°, and west of the foot hills of the Sierra Nevada, the forests of California are limited to some scattering groves of oak in the valleys and along the borders of the streams, and of red wood on the ridges and in the gorges of the hills—sometimes extending into the plains. Some of the hills are covered with dwarf shrubs, which may be used as fuel. With these exceptions, the whole territory presents a surface without trees or shrubbery. It is covered, however, with various species of grass, and for many miles from the coast with wild oats, which, in the valleys, grow most luxuriantly. These grasses and oats mature and ripen early in the dry season, and soon cease to protect the soil from the scorching rays of the sun. As the summer advances, the moisture in the atmosphere and the earth, to a considerable depth, soon becomes exhausted ; and the radiation of heat, from the extensive naked plains and hill sides, is very great.

The cold, dry currents of air from the northeast, after passing the Rocky Mountains and the Sierra Nevada, descend to the Pacific, and absorb the moisture of the atmosphere, to a great distance from the land. The cold air from the mountains, and that which accompanies the great ocean current from the northwest, thus become united, and vast banks of fog are generated, which, when driven by the wind, has a penetrating, or *cutting* effect on the human skin, much more uncomfortable than would be felt in the humid atmosphere of the Atlantic, at a much lower temperature.

As the sun rises from day to day, week after week, and month after month, in unclouded brightness during the dry season, and pours down his unbroken rays on the dry, unprotected surface of the country, the heat becomes so much greater inland than it is on the ocean, that an under current of cold air, bringing the fog with it, rushes over the coast range of hills, and through their numerous passes, toward the interior.

Every day, as the heat, inland, attains a sufficient temperature, the cold, dry wind from the ocean commences to blow   This is usually from

11 to 1 o'clock; and as the day advances the wind increases and continues to blow till late at night. When the vacuum is filled, or the equilibrium of the atmosphere restored, the wind ceases; a perfect calm prevails until about the same hour the following day, when the same process commences and progresses as before, and these phenomena are of daily occurrence, with few exceptions, throughout the dry season.

These cold winds and fogs render the climate at San Francisco, and all along the coast of California, except the extreme southern portion of it, probably more uncomfortable, to those not accustomed to it, in summer than in winter.

A few miles inland, where the heat of the sun modifies and softens the wind from the ocean, the climate is moderate and delightful. The heat in the middle of the day is not so great as to retard labor, or render exercise in the open air uncomfortable. The nights are cool and pleasant. This description of climate prevails in all the valleys along the coast range, and extends throughout the country, north and south, as far eastward as the valley of the Sacramento and San Joaquin. In this vast plain the sea breeze loses its influence, and the degree of heat in the middle of the day, during the summer months, is much greater than is known on the Atlantic coast in the same latitudes. It is dry, however, and probably not more oppressive. On the foot hills of the Sierra Nevada, and especially in the deep ravines of the streams, the thermometer frequently ranges from 110° to 115° in the shade, during three or four hours of the day, say from 11 to 3 o'clock. In the evening as the sun declines, the radiation of heat ceases. The cool dry atmosphere from the mountains spreads over the whole country, and renders the nights cool and invigorating.

I have been kindly furnished by Surgeon General Lawson, U. S. Army, with thermometrical observations, taken at the places in California, viz: At San Francisco, by Assistant Surgeon W. C. Parker, for six months embracing the last quarter of 1847, and the first quarter of 1848. The monthly mean temperature was as follows: October, 57°; November, 49°; December, 50°; January, 49°; February, 50°; March, 51°.

At Monterey, in latitude 36° 38' north, and longitude 121° west, on the coast, about one degree and a half south of San Francisco, by Assistant Surgeon W. S. King, for seven months, from May to November inclusive. The monthly mean temperature was: May, 56°; June, 59°; July, 62°; August, 59°; September, 58°; October, 60°; November, 56°.

At Los Angelos, latitude 34° 7', longitude west 118° 7', by Assistant Surgeon John S. Griffin, for ten months—from June, 1847, to March, 1848, inclusive. The monthly mean temperature was: June, 73°; July, 74°; August, 75°; September, 75°; October, 69°; November, 59°; December, 60°. This place is about forty miles from the coast.

At San Diego, latitude 32° 45', longitude west 117° 11', by Assistant Surgeon J. D. Summers, for the following three months of 1849, viz.: July, monthly mean temperature, 71°; August, 75°; September, 70°.

At Suttersville, on the Sacramento River, latitude 38° 32' north, longitude west 121° 34', by Assistant Surgeon R. Murray, for the following months of 1849: July, monthly mean temperature 73°; August, 70°; September, 65°; October, 65°.

These observations show a remarkably high temperature at San Francisco during the six months from October to March inclusive; a variation of only eight degrees in the monthly mean, and a mean temperature for the six months of 51 degrees.

At Monterey we find the mean monthly temperature from May to November, inclusive, varying only six degrees, and the mean temperature of the seven months to have been 58°. If we take the three summer months, the mean heat was 60°. The mean of the three winter months was a little over 49°; showing a mean difference, on that part of the coast, of only 11° between summer and winter.

The mean temperature of San Francisco, for the three winter months, was precisely the same as at Monterey—a little over 49°.

As these cities are only about one degree and a half distant from each other, and both situated near the ocean, the temperature at both, in summer, may very reasonably be supposed to be as nearly similar as the thermometer shows it to be in winter.

The mean temperature of July, August and September, at San Diego, only 3° 53' south of Monterey, was 72°. The mean temperature of the same months at Monterey was a little over 59°, showing a mean difference of 13°.

This would seem to indicate that the cold ocean current is thrown off from the southern part of the coast by Point Conception, and the islands south of it; and consequently its influence on the climate of San Diego is much less than at Monterey and San Francisco.

At Los Angelos, forty miles distant from the coast, the mean temperature of the three months is 74°; and of the three autumn months 67°; of the three winter months 57°.

At Suttersville, about one hundred and thirty miles from the ocean, and 4° north of Los Angelos, the mean temperature of August, September and October was 67°. The mean temperature of the same months at Monterey was 59°; showing a difference of 8° between the sea-coast and the interior, on nearly the same parallel of latitude. A much greater difference would undoubtedly appear if we had observation for the spring and summer months at Suttersville and the gold mines.

These variations in the climate of California account for the various and conflicting opinions and statements respecting it.

A stranger arriving at San Francisco in summer is annoyed by the cold winds and fogs, and pronounces the climate intolerable. A few months will modify if not banish his dislike, and he will not fail to appreciate the beneficial effects of a cool, bracing atmosphere. Those who approach California overland, through the passes of the mountains, find the heat of summer, in the middle of the day, greater than they have been accustomed to, and therefore many complain of it.

Those who take up their residence in the valleys which are situated between the great plain of the Sacramento and San Joaquin, and the coast range of hills, find the climate, especially in the dry season, as healthful and pleasant as it is possible for any climate to be which possesses sufficient heat to mature the cereal grains and edible roots of the temperate zone.

The division of the year into two distinct seasons—dry and wet—impresses those who have been accustomed to the variable climate of the Atlantic States unfavorably. The dry appearance of the country in summer and the difficulty of moving about in winter seem to impose serious difficulties in the way of agricultural prosperity, while the many and decided advantages resulting from the mildness of winter, and the bright, clear weather of summer, are not appreciated. These will appear when I come to speak of the productions of California. We ought not to be surprised at the dislike which the immigrants frequently express to the climate. It is so unlike that from which they come, that they cannot readily appreciate its advantages, or become reconciled to its extremes of dry and wet.

If a native of California were to go to New England in winter, and see the ground frozen and covered with snow, the streams with ice, and find himself in a temperature many degrees colder than he had ever felt before, he would probably be as much surprised that people could or would live in so inhospitable a region, as any immigrant ever has been at what he has seen or felt in California.

So much are our opinions influenced by early impressions, the vicissitudes of the seasons with which we are familiar, love of country, home and kindred, that we ought never to hazard a hasty opinion, when we come in contact with circumstances entirely different from those to which we have all our lives been accustomed.

SOIL.

The valleys which are situated parallel to the coast range, and those which extend eastwardly in all directions among the hills, toward the great plain of the Sacramento, are of unsurpassed fertility.

They have a deep, black, alluvial soil, which has the appearance of having been deposited when they were covered with water. The idea is strengthened by the fact that the rising grounds on the borders of these valleys, and many hills of moderate elevation have a soil precisely like that of the adjoining plains.

This soil is so porous, that it remains perfectly unbroken by gullies, notwithstanding the great quantity of water which falls in it annually during the wet season. The land in the northern part of the territory on the Trinity and other rivers, and on the borders of Clear Lake, as far as it has been examined, is said to be remarkably fertile.

The great valley of the Sacramento and San Joaquin has evidently been, at some remote period, the bed of a lake; and those rivers which drain it, present the appearance of having cut their channels through the alluvial deposit after it had been formed. In fact, it is not possible that they could have been instrumental in forming the plain through which they pass. Their head-waters come from the extreme ends of the valley, north and south ; and, were it not for the supply of water received from the streams which flow into them from the Sierra Nevada, their beds would be almost, if not quite, dry in the summer months. The soil is very rich, and, with a proper system of drainage and embankment, would, undoubtedly, be capable of producing any crop, except sugar cane, now cultivated in the Atlantic States of the Union.

There are many beautiful valleys and rich hill sides among the foot hills of the Sierra Nevada, which, when the profits of labor in mining shall be reduced, so as to cause its application to agriculture, will probably support a large population. There is said to be a rich belt of well-timbered and watered country extending the whole length of the gold region between it and the Sierra Nevada, some twenty miles in width. There is no information sufficiently accurate respecting the eastern slope of the great snowy range to enable us to form any opinion of its general character or soil. Some of its valleys have been visited by miners, who represent them as fully equal to any portion of the country to the westward of it.

The great valley of the Colorado, situated between the Sierra Madre and the Sierra Nevada, is but little known. It is inhabited by numerous tribes of savages, who manifest the most decided hostility toward the whites, and have hitherto prevented any explorations of their country, and do not permit emigrants to pass through it. Therefore parties from Santa Fe, on their way to California, are compelled to make a circuit of near a thousand miles northward to the Salt Lake, or about the same distance southward by the route of the Gila. Although this valley is little known, there are indications that it is fertile and valuable.

The name of the river "Colorado" is descriptive of its waters ; they are as deeply colored as those of the Missouri or Red River, while those of the Gila, which we know flows through barren lands, are clear.

It would seem impossible for a large river to collect sediment enough in a sandy, barren soil to color its waters so deeply as to give it a name among those who first discovered and have since visited its shores. The probability, therefore, is, that this river flows through an alluvial valley of great fertility, which has never been explored. This conjecture is strengthened by the fact that the Indians who inhabit it are hostile, and oppose, as far as they can, all persons who attempt to enter or explore it. This has been their uniform course of conduct respecting all portions of the continent which have been fertile, abounding in game and the spontaneous productions of the earth.

As this valley is situated in the direct route from Santa Fe to California, its thorough exploration becomes a matter of very great importance, especially as it is highly probable that the elevated regions to the north of it, covered with snow during most of the year, will force the line of the great National Railway to the Pacific through some portion of it.

The soil I have described situated west of the Sierra Nevada, and embracing the plain of the Sacramento and San Joaquin, covers an area, as nearly as I can estimate, of between fifty and sixty thousand square miles, and would, under a proper system of cultivation, be capable of supporting a population equal to that of Ohio or New York at the present time.

PRODUCTS OF CALIFORNIA.

Previous to the treaty of peace with Mexico, and the discovery of gold, the exportable products of the country consisted almost exclusively of hides and tallow. The Californians were a pastoral people, and paid much more attention to the raising of horses and cattle than the cultivation of the soil.

Wheat, barley, maize, beans and edible roots, were cultivated in sufficient quantity for home consumption, but, as far as I am informed, not for exportation. At that time a full-grown ox, steer, or cow, was worth about two dollars. Beef cattle, delivered on the navigable waters of the bay of San Francisco, are now worth from $20 to $30 per head; horses, formerly worth from $5 to $10, are now valued at $60 to $150. The destruction of cattle for their hides and tallow has now entirely ceased, in consequence of the demand for beef. This demand will of course increase with the population; and it would seem that, in a very few years, there will be none to supply the market.

If we estimate the number of cattle, now in California, at 500,000 head, which is believed to be about the number—and the population at 120,000, for the year 1850—a low estimate—and suppose it to increase 100,000 per annum, there will be in the Territory or State, in 1854, 520,000 people.

If we adopt the estimate of those well acquainted with the demand, of half a beef, on an average, to each inhabitant, it appears there will be a consumption, in 1850, of 60,000 head; in 1851, of 110,000; in 1852, of 160,000; in 1853, of 210,000; in 1854, of 260,000. Making an aggregate of 800,000, which would absorb all the present stock, with is natural increase.

This is a very important matter, as connected with the amount of supply which that country will ultimately require from the Atlantic States of the Union. There is no other country on earth which has, or will ever possess, the means of supplying so great a demand.

It is now a well-established fact among the emigrants to California, that oxen possess greater powers of endurance than mules or horses; that they will perform the distance with loaded wagons in less time, and come in at the end of the journey in better condition.

Cows are now driven in considerable numbers from Missouri, and the time cannot be far distant when cattle from the western States will be driven annually by tens of thousands to supply this new market.

If California increases in population as fast as the most moderate estimate would lead us to believe, it will not be five years before she will require more than 100,000 head of beef cattle per annum, from some quarter, to supply the wants of her people.

It must not be supposed that salt provisions may supply this vast demand. Those who have attempted to live on such food, during the dry season, have been attacked with scurvy and other cutaneous diseases of which many have died.

There is no climate in the world where fresh meat and vegetables are more essential to human health. In fact they are indispensable.

It must not be inferred that cattle driven across the plains and mountains, from the western States, will be fit for beef on their arrival in California. But one winter and spring on the luxuriant pastures of that country will put them in a condition which would render them acceptable in any Atlantic market.

These grazing grounds are extensive enough to support five times as many cattle as may be *annually* required; therefore, there will be no scarcity of food for them.

I am acquainted with a drover who left California in December last with the intention of bringing in ten thousand sheep from New Mexico. This shows that the flocks and herds east of the Rocky Mountains are looked to already as the source from which the markets on the Pacific are to be supplied.

The climate and soil of California are well suited to the growth of wheat, barley, rye and oats. The temperature along the coast is too cool for the successful culture of maize, as a field crop. The fact that oats, the species which is cultivated in the Atlantic States, are annually self-sowed and produced on all the plains and hills along the coast, and as far inland as the sea breeze has a marked influence on the climate, is sufficient proof that all the cereal grains may be successfully cultivated without the aid of *irrigation*.

It is quite true that *this auxiliary* was extensively employed at the missions, and undoubtedly increased the product of all crops to which it was applied, as it will in any country on earth if skilfully used. This does not prove, however, that it was *essentially necessary* to the production of an ample reward to the husbandman. The experience of all the old inhabitants is sufficient evidence of this. If their imperfect mode of culture secured satisfactory returns, it is reasonable to presume that a more perfect system would produce much greater results. There is abundant evidence to prove that, in the rich alluvial valleys, wheat and barley have produced from forty to sixty bushels from one bushel of seed, *without irrigation*.

Irish potatoes, turnips, onions, in fact all the edible roots known and cultivated in the Atlantic States, are produced in great perfection. In all the valleys east of the coast range of hills the climate is sufficiently warm to mature crops of Indian corn, rice, and probably tobacco.

The cultivation of the grape has attracted much attention at the missions, among the residents of towns, and the rural population, and been attended with much success, wherever it has been attempted. The dry season secures the fruit from those diseases which are so common in the Atlantic States, and it attains very great perfection.

The wine made from it is of excellent quality, very palatable, and can be produced in any quantity. The grapes are delicious, and produced with very little labor. When taken from the vines in bunches and suspended in a dry room, by the stems, they become partially dry, retain their flavor, and remain several weeks, perhaps months, without decay.

Apples, pears and peaches are cultivated with facility, and there is no reason to doubt that all the fruits of the Atlantic States can be produced in great plenty and perfection.

The grasses are very luxuriant and nutritious, affording excellent pasture. The oats, which spring up the whole length of the sea coast, and from forty to sixty miles inland, render the cultivation of that crop entirely unnecessary, and yield a very great quantity of nutritious food for horses, cattle, and sheep. The dry season matures, and I may say, cures these grasses and oats, so that they remain in an excellent state of preservation during the summer and autumn, and afford an ample supply of forage. While the whole surface of the country appears parched, and vegetation destroyed, the numerous flocks and herds, which roam over it, continue in excellent condition.

Although the mildness of the winter months and the fertility of the soil secure to California very decided agricultural advantages, it is admitted that *irrigation* would be of very great importance, and necessarily increase the products of the soil in quantity and variety, during the greater part of the dry season. It should, therefore, be encouraged by Government, in the survey and disposition of the public lands, as far as practicable.

The farmer derives some very important benefits from the dry season. His crops in harvest time are never injured by rain; he can with perfect confidence permit them to remain in his fields as long after they have been gathered as his convenience may require; he has no fears that they will be injured by wet or unfavorable weather. Hence it is that many who have long been accustomed to that climate, prefer it to the changeable weather east of the Rocky Mountains.

As already stated, the forests of California, south of latitude 39°, and west of the foot hills of the Sierra Nevada, are limited to detached, scattering groves of oak in the valleys, and of red-wood on the ridges and on the gorges of the hills.

It can be of no practical use to speculate on the causes which have denuded so large an extent of country, further than to ascertain whether the soil is or is not favorable to the growth of forest trees.

When the dry season sets in, the entire surface is covered with a luxuriant growth of grass and oats, which, as the summer advances, becomes perfectly dry. The remains of all dead trees and shrubs also become dry. These materials, therefore, are very combustible, and usually take fire in the latter part of summer and beginning of autumn, which commonly passes over the whole country, destroying in its course, the young shrubs and trees. In fact, it seems to be the same process which has destroyed or prevented the growth of forest trees on the prairies of the western States, and not any quality in the soil unfriendly to their growth.

The absence of timber and the continuance of the dry season are apt to be regarded by farmers, on first going into the country, as irremediable defects, and as presenting obstacles almost insurmountable to the successful progress of agriculture. A little experience will modify these opinions.

It is soon ascertained that the soil will produce abundantly without manure ; that flocks and herds sustain themselves through the winter without being fed at the farmyard, and, consequently, no labor is necessary to provide forage for them ; that ditches are easily dug, which present very good barriers for the protection of crops, until live fences can be planted and have time to grow. Forest trees may be planted with little labor, and in very few years attain a sufficient size for building and fencing purposes. Time may be usefully employed in sowing various grain and root crops during the wet or winter season. There is no weather cold enough to destroy root crops, and, therefore, it is not necessary to gather them. They can be used or sold from the field where they grow. The labor, therefore, required in most of the old States to fell the forests, clear the land of rubbish, and prepare it for seed, may here be applied to other objects.

All these things, together with the *perfect security of all crops, in harvest time from injury by wet weather*, are probably sufficient to meet any expense which may be incurred in irrigation, or caused, for a time, by a scanty supply of timber.

In the northern part of the Territory, above latitude 39°, and on the hills, which rise from the great plain of the Sacramento and San Joaquin, to the foot of the Sierra Nevada, the forests of timber are beautiful and extensive, and would, if brought into use, be sufficiently productive to supply the wants of the southern and western portions of the State.

I have spoken of the agricultural products and resources of the country, without reference to the remarkable state of things caused by the discovery of gold, which, it is probable will postpone for an indefinite time all efforts to improve the soil. As long as laborers can earn fifteen dollars or more per day, in collecting gold, they can very well afford to import their supplies from countries where the wages of labor are not more than from fifty cents to one dollar per day. It is not, therefore, to be supposed that the soil will be cultivated more than the production of vegetables, fruits, and other articles so perishable in their nature that they cannot be brought from a great distance, will require.

To secure this important market for the products and manufactures of the States east of the Rocky Mountains is undoubtedly an object of the greatest importance. It will be considered in its proper place.

PUBLIC DOMAIN.

The extent and value of the public lands, suitable for agricultural purposes in California, cannot be ascertained with any degree of accuracy until some very important preliminary questions shall have been settled.

It is not known whether the Jesuits who founded the mission, or their successors, the Franciscans, ever did, or do now hold any title from the Spanish crown to the lands which they occupied. Nor has any investigation been made to ascertain how far those titles, if they ever existed, have been invalidated by the acts of the priests, or the decrees of the Mexican government.

A superficial view of the matter would be very apt to lead to the supposition that the Jesuits, so celebrated for wisdom and cunning, would not fail to secure that which, at that time, would probably have been obtained by merely asking for it—a royal decree, granting to them all the lands they might require in that remote country for ecclesiastical purposes. There have been some intimations to that effect, but nothing is distinctly known. These missions embrace within their limits some of the most valuable lands in the Territory, and it is very important that it should be ascertained whether they belong to the government, or may justly be claimed by individuals.

Most of the land fit for cultivation south of latitude 39°, and west of the valley of the Sacramento and San Joaquin, is claimed under, what purport to be, grants from the Mexican government.

On most of these grants the minerals and metals are reserved to the government—conditions were coupled with many of them which have not been complied with. In others, the boundaries described embrace two or three times as much land as the grant conveys.

The Mexican law required all grants made by the Provisional Government, with few exceptions, to be confirmed by the Supreme Government. The great distance which separated them, and the unfrequent or difficult means of communication, made a compliance with the law so expensive and tardy, that it came to be almost disregarded.

There were other causes which led to this neglect.

Previous to the treaty with Mexico and the immigration of American citizens to that country, land was not regarded as of much value, except for grazing purposes. There was room enough for all. Therefore the claimants or proprietors did not molest each other, or inquire into the validity of titles.

These extensive grants are described by natural boundaries, such as mountains, bays and promontories, which, in many instances might allow of a variation of several miles in the establishment of a corner with chain and compass.

By the treaty of Guadalupe Hidalgo, the United States purchased all the rights and interests of Mexico to and in California. This purchase not only embraced all the lands which had not been granted by Mexico, but all the reserved minerals and metals, and also the revisionary rights which might accrue to Mexico from a want of compliance on the part of

10*

the grantees with the conditions of their grants, *or a want of perfection in the grants.*

It will be perceived that this is a subject of very great importance, not only to the people of California, but to the United States, and calls for prompt and efficient action on the part of the government. It is believed that the appointment of competent commissioners, fully empowered to investigate these titles, in a spirit of kindness toward the claimants, with power to confirm such titles as justice may seem to demand, or with instructions to report their proceedings and awards to Congress, for confirmation or rejection, will be the best and perhaps the only satisfactory mode of adjusting this complex and difficult question.

The lands in the northern part of the Territory, above the 39°, have not been explored or granted. They are supposed to embrace an area of about twenty millions of acres, a large portion of which is doubtless valuable for its timber and soil.

Comparatively few grants have been obtained in the great valley of the Sacramento and San Joaquin. This vast tract, therefore, containing, as is estimated, from twelve to fifteen millions of acres, belongs mostly to the government. South of this valley, and west of the Colorado, within the limits of California, as indicated in her constitution, there are said to be extensive tracts of valuable unappropriated land, and on investigation it will probably appear that there are many of them in detached bodies, which have not been granted.

do not speak of the gold region, embracing the entire foot hills of the Sierra Nevada, some five hundred miles long and sixty miles broad, in connexion with the public domain, which may be embraced in the general land system for sale and settlement, for reasons which will be hereafter assigned.

The survey of the public lands on a system suited to the interests of the country is a matter of very great importance. In the inhabited portions of the Territory the boundaries of Mexican grants, running as they do in all directions, will render the system of surveys by parallels of latitude and longitude quite impracticable.

In all parts of the country irrigation is desirable, and its benefits should be secured as far as possible by suitable surveys and legal regutions. Most of the valleys are watered by streams sufficiently large to be rendered very useful. It would, therefore, seem wise to lay off the land in conformity to the course of the hills and streams which bound and drain the valleys.

A system of drainage, which would also secure irrigation, is absolutely necessary to give value to the great plain of the Sacramento and San Joaquin. This valley is so extensive and level, that if the rivers passing through it were never to overflow their banks, the rain which falls in winter would render a greater portion of it unfit for cultivation. The foundation of such a system can only be established in the survey and sale of the land.

This can be done by laying out canals and drains at suitable distances, and in proper directions and leaving wide margins to the rivers, that they may have plenty of room to increase their channels when their waters shall be confined within them by embankments.

It would be well also to regulate the price of these lands so as to meet, in some degree, the expense of draining them.

This system would, when agriculture shall become a pursuit in California, make this valley one of the most beautiful and productive portions of the Union.

COMMERCIAL RESOURCES.

The commercial resources of California are, at present, founded entirely on her *metallic wealth*—her vast mineral treasures remaining undeveloped, and her fertile soil almost wholly neglected; and this must continue to be the case as long as labor, employed in collecting gold, shall be more profitable than in any other pursuit which can furnish the sinews of commerce.

The day is probably not distant, however, when her minerals, especially the quicksilver mines, will be extensively and profitably worked.

Gold is the product of the country, and is immediately available, in an uncoined state, for all the purposes of exchange. It is not there, as in other countries where the productions of the earth and of art are sent to markets—foreign or domestic—to be exchanged for the precious metals or other articles of value. There, gold not only supplies the medium of domestic trade, but of foreign commerce.

At first view, this state of things would seem to be unfavorable to all extensive intercourse with other parts of the world, because of the want of return freights of *home production* for the vast number of vessels which will arrive with supplies.

These vessels, however, making no calculations on return cargoes, will estimate the entire profits of the voyage on their outward freights, and become, on their arrival, willing carriers for a comparatively small consideration.

This tendency in the course of trade, it would seem, must make San Francisco a warehouse for the supply, to a certain extent, of all the ports of the Pacific, American, Asiatic, and the Islands.

Almost every article now exported by them finds a ready market in California, and the establishment of a mint will bring there also the silver bullion, amounting to more than ten millions per annum, from the west coast of Mexico, and, perhaps, ultimately from Chili and Peru, to be assayed and coined.

Vessels bound round Cape Horn, with cargoes for markets on the American coast of the Pacific, can, by taking advantage of the southeast trade winds, and "standing broad-off the Cape," make the voyage to San Francisco in as short a time as they can to Valparaiso or any port south of California. Vessels have sailed from our Atlantic ports to San Francisco in less than one hundred days, and they have been, in more than one instance, over one hundred and twenty days in going from Panama to San Francisco.

This astonishing difference, in time and distance, was caused by the course of the winds and the "gulf-stream" of the Pacific, mentioned in my remarks on the climate of California.

The vessels from our Atlantic ports took advantage of the winds by steering *from the Cape* as far into the Pacific as to be enabled to take a course west of the gulf-stream in sailing northward, thus availing themselves, first of the southeast, then of the northwest " trades," and avoiding opposing currents.

The vessels from Panama were kept back by calms, adverse winds, and currents. It will be perceived, therefore, that there can be no inducement for vessels bound round Cape Horn, with mixed or assorted cargoes, to stop at Valparaiso, Callao, Guayaquil, or any other port on the west coast, because the exports of all those places will seek a market at San Francisco ; and their supply of merchandize, as *return freight*, will be delivered at less expense than it can be by vessels direct from Atlantic ports, American or European. This tendency of trade to concentrate at San Francisco will be aided by the course of exchange.

Gold dust is worth but $17 per ounce in Chili. It is worth $18 at the United States Mint. If, therefore, a merchant of Valparaiso has ten thousand ounces in San Francisco, received in payment for lumber, barley, flour, or other produce, and desires an invoice of goods from the United States or Europe, he will gain $10,000 at the outset, by sending his gold to New York, besides saving something on the freight and insurance, and at least one month's interest.

The countries on the west coast of America have no exports which find a market in China, or other ports of Asia. San Francisco will therefore become not only the mart of these exports, but also of the products and manufactures of India required in exchange for them, which must be paid for, principally in gold coin or gold dust. Neither gold coin nor gold dust will answer as a remittance to China. Gold, in China, is not currency in any shape, nor is it received in payment of import duties, or taxes on land, or on the industry of the people.

The value of pure gold in China is not far from $14 the ounce. Hence, the importer of manufactures and products of India into San Francisco will remit the gold coin or dust direct to New York, for investment in sterling bills on London. These bills will be sent to London, and placed to the credit of the firm in China from whom the merchandise had been received, and who, on learning of the remittance having gone forward to their agents, will draw a *six months' sight bill* for the amount, which will sell in China at the rate of four shillings and *two* pence or *three* pence per dollar.

I have a statement before me from one of the most eminent merchants and bankers of New York, who was for many years engaged extensively in the India trade, which shows that the profit or gain on ten thousand ounces of gold thus remitted would be $34,434 44

And that the loss on the same quantity, sent direct to China,
    would be 15,600 00

Total difference in profit and loss in favor of the remittance
    to New York, ... $50,034 44

It will thus be perceived, that nature has so arranged the winds and currents of the Pacific, and disposed of her vast treasures in the hills and mountains of California, as to give to the harbor of San Francisco the control of the commerce of that ocean, as far as it may be connected with the west coast of America.

Important as the commerce of the Pacific undoubtedly is, and will be, to California, it cannot now, nor will it ever compare in magnitude and value to the domestic trade between her and the older States of the Union.

Two years ago California did not probably contain more than 15,000 people. That portion of it which has since been so wonderfully peopled by American citizens, was, comparatively, without resources, and not supplied with the common comforts of shelter afforded by a forest country.

Notwithstanding the great distances emigrants have been compelled to travel to reach the Territory, more than 100,000 have overcome all difficulties and spread themselves over its hills and plains.

They have been supplied from distances as great as they themselves have passed, with not only the necessaries, but the comforts and many of the luxuries of life. Houses have been imported from China, Chili, and the Atlantic States of the Union. All the materials required in building cities and towns have been added to the wants of a people so numerous, destitute and remote from the sources of supply.

These wants will exist as long as emigration continues to flow into the country, and labor employed in collecting gold shall be more profitable than its application to agriculture, the mechanic arts, and the great variety of pursuits which are fostered and sustained in other civilized communities.

This may be shown, by mentioning the prices of a few articles. Last summer and autumn, lumber was sold in San Francisco at $300 to $400 per thousand feet. At Stockton and Sacramento City, at $500 to $600. At these prices, it could be made in the Territory, and many persons were engaged in the business. I perceive, by recent accounts, that the price had fallen at San Francisco to $75; at this price it *cannot* be made where labor is from $10 to $15 per day, and the difficulties attending its manufacture are much greater than in the Atlantic States. Lumber can be delivered in our large lumber markets for an *average* of the various qualities of $16, and freighted to San Francisco for $24, making $40 per thousand feet. This price would cause the manufacture of it in California to be abandoned. We may add $20 per thousand to meet any increase of price in the article itself, or in the freight, and the result would be the same.

It is probable that the demand, for several years to come, will not be less than twenty millions of feet per annum, which, at $40 per thousand, will be $8,000,000.

When California comes to have a population of 200,000, which she will have before the close of the present year, she will require near half a million of barrels of flour from some quarter, and no country can supply it as good and cheap as the old States of the Union. Including freight and insurance, this may be set down as an item of about $5,000,000. The article of clothing, allowing $20 to each person, would be $4,000,000.

There is no pretension to accuracy in these items, and they may be estimated too high, but it is quite as probable they are too low.

We have no data on which to found a calculation of what the value of the trade between the States east of the Rocky Mountains and California will be during the current year. I will venture the opinion, however, that it will not fall short of $25,000,000. It may go far beyond that sum. At present, I can perceive no cause which will retard or diminish emigration.

If the movement shall continue five years, our commerce with that Territory may reach $100,000,000 per annum. This is doubtless a startling sum, but it must be borne in mind that we have to build cities and towns, supply machinery for mining, coal for domestic purposes, and steam navigation, and all the multifarious articles used in providing the comforts and luxuries of life, for half a million of people, who will have transferred themselves to a country which is to produce, comparatively, nothing except minerals and the precious metals, and whose pursuits will enable them to purchase, at any cost, whatever may be necessary for their purposes.

It is difficult to imagine or calculate the effect which will be produced on all the industrial pursuits of the people of the old States of the Union, by this withdrawal from them of a half a million of producers, who, in their new homes and new pursuits, will *give existence* to a commerce almost equal in value to our foreign trade. Let no one, therefore, suppose he is not interested in the welfare of California. As well may he believe his interests would not be influenced by closing our ports and cutting off intercourse with all the world.

The distance round Cape Horn is so great that breadstuffs and many other articles of food deteriorate, and many others are so perishable in their nature that they would decay on the passage. This would be the case particularly with all kinds of vegetables and undried fruits. Until some more speedy mode of communication shall be established by which produce can be transferred, the farmers and planters of the old States will not realize the full value of this new market on the Pacific.

Many other important interests will be kept back, especially the consumption of coal. The American steamers now on the ocean, those on their way there and others shortly to be sent out will consume not far from one hundred thousand tons of coal per annum. The scarcity of wood in California will bring coal into general use as fuel as soon as it can be obtained at reasonable prices. Suppose there may be three years hence forty thousand houses, which shall consume five tons each per annum. This, with the steamers, would be a consumption of three hundred thousand tons. If delivered at $20 per ton it would compete successfully with the coal from Vancouver's Island and New Holland and amount to $6,000,000.

The construction of a railroad across the Isthmus of Panama would secure the market for these articles against all competition.

Some idea may be formed of the demand for them from the prices paid in San Francisco last autumn. Coal was sold at $60 to $100 per ton;

potatoes $16 per bushel; turnips and onions for 25 to 62½ cts. each; eggs from $10 to $12 per dozen.

The distance from Chagres to New York has recently been run in seven days. The same speed would carry a steamboat from Panama to San Francisco in ten days. Allow three days to convey freight across the Isthmus, on a railway, and both passengers and freight will be conveyed from New York to San Francisco in twenty days.

This celerity of movement would secure for American produce the entire market of California. Sailing vessels may be successfully employed between our Atlantic and Gulf ports and the terminus of the railway on this side of the Isthmus; and *propellers* from Panama to San Francisco. These latter vessels will be found peculiarly suited to that trade; they can use their steam through the calms of the Bay of Panama, and against head winds and currents going north, and their sails with favorable winds and currents coming south.

These modes of conveyance, in connexion with the railroad across the Isthmus, would be sufficiently expeditious and economical to turn the tide of commerce, between the Atlantic and Pacific States of the Union, into that channel. The tendency of our commerce on the Pacific to promote the employment of ocean steamers is of much importance as connected with the defence of our extensive line of coast from latitude 32° to 49°, the protection of the whale fishery, and other branches of trade on that ocean. The establishment of a line of heavy steamers to China would promote all these objects; increase our intercourse with the country, and probably be the means of opening communications with Japan. Money wisely employed in promoting these objects, it is believed, would add more to the power and prosperity of the country than its expenditure on any *general system* of fortification at the present prices of labor and materials. There is one point, however, of such vast importance that no time should be lost in taking the necessary steps to render it perfectly impregnable—that is the entrance to the harbor of San Francisco. On the strength of the works which may be erected to defend that passage will depend the safety of California in a time of war with a maritime power. Permit a hostile fleet to cast anchor in the harbor of San Francisco and the country would be virtually conquered.

The coast has not been surveyed, nor has its outline bean correctly ascertained. There are many rocks above and below the water-line, and small islands not mentioned or indicated on any chart, which render navigation near the land, especially at night, extremely dangerous.

An accurate survey of the coast, to commence at the most important points, the construction of light-houses, and the placing of buoys in proper positions, are objects of much importance, and, it is not doubted, will attract the early attention of government.

METALLIC AND MINERAL WEALTH.

The gold region of California is between four hundred and five hundred miles long, and from forty to fifty miles broad, following the line of the Sierra Nevada. Further discoveries may, and probably will, increase the area. It embraces within its limits those extensive ranges of hills which rise on the eastern border of the plain of the Sacramento and San Joaquin, and extending eastwardly from fifty to sixty miles, they attain an elevation of about four thousand feet, and terminate at the base of the main ridge of the Sierra Nevada. There are numerous streams which have their sources in the springs of the Sierra, and receive the water from its melting snows, and that which falls in rain during the wet season.

These streams form rivers, which have cut their channels through the ranges of foot hills westwardly to the plain, and disembogue into the Sacramento and San Joaquin. These rivers are from ten to fifteen, and probably some of them twenty miles apart.

The principal formation or substratum in these hills is talcose slate; the superstratum, sometimes penetrating to a great depth, is quartz. This, however, does not cover the entire face of the country, but extends in large bodies in various directions—is found in masses and small fragments on the surface, and seen along the ravines, and in the mountains overhanging the rivers, and in the hill sides in its orignal beds. It crops out in the valleys and on the tops of the hills, and forms a striking feature of the entire country over which it extends. From innumerable evidence and indications, it has come to be the universally admitted opinion among the miners and intelligent men who have examined this region, that the *gold, whether in detached particles and in pieces, or in veins, was created in combination with the quartz.* Gold is not found on the surface of the country, presenting the appearance of having been thrown up and scattered in all directions by volcanic action. It is only found in particular localities, and attended by peculiar circumstances and indications. It is found in the bars and shoals of the rivers, in ravines, and in what are called the dry diggings.

The rivers, in forming their channels, or breaking their way through the hills, have come in contact with the quartz containing the gold veins, and by constant attrition cut the gold into fine flakes and dust, and it is found among the sand and gravel of their beds at those places where the swiftness of the current reduces it, in the dry season, to the narrowest possible limits, and where a wide margin is, consequently, left on each side, over which the water rushes, during the wet season, with great force.

As the velocity of some streams is greater than others, so is the gold found in fine or coarse particles, apparently corresponding to the degree of attrition to which it has been exposed. The water from the hills and upper valleys, in finding its way to the rivers, has cut deep ravines, and, wherever it came in contact with the quartz, has dissolved or crumbled it in pieces.

In the dry season these channels are mostly without water, and gold is found in the beds and margins of many of them in large quantities, but in a much coarser state than in the rivers; owing, undoubtedly, to the moderate flow and temporary continuance of the current, which has reduced it to smooth shapes, not unlike pebbles, but had not sufficient force to reduce it to flakes or dust.

The dry diggings are places where quartz containing gold has cropped out, and been disintegrated, crumbled to fragments, pebbles and dust, by the action of water and the atmosphere. The gold has been left as it was made, in all imaginable shapes; in pieces of all sizes, and from one grain to several pounds in weight. The evidences that it was created in combination with quartz are too numerous and striking to admit of doubt or cavil. *They are found in combination in large quantities.*

A very large proportion of the pieces of gold found in these situations have more or less quartz adhering to them. In many specimens they are so combined they cannot be separated without reducing the whole mass to powder and subjecting it to the action of quicksilver.

This gold, not having been exposed to the attrition of a strong current of water, retains, in a great degree, its original conformation.

These diggings, in some places, spread over valleys of considerable extent, which have the appearance of alluvion, formed by washings from the adjoining hills, of decomposed quartz and slate earth, and vegetable matter.

In addition to these facts it is beyond doubt true, that several vein-mines have been taken, showing the minute connection between the gold and the rock, and indicating a value hitherto unknown in gold-mining.

These veins do not present the appearance of places where gold may have been lodged by some violent eruption. It is combined with the quartz, in all imaginable forms and degrees of richness.

The rivers present very striking and, it would seem, conclusive evidence respecting the quantity of gold remaining undiscovered in the quartz veins. It is not probable that the gold in the dry diggings, and that in the rivers—the former in lumps, the latter in dust—was created by different processes. That which is found in the rivers has undoubtedly been cut or worn from the veins in the rock, with which their currents have come in contact. All of them appear to be equally rich. This is shown by the fact that a laboring man may collect nearly as much in one river as he can in another. They intersect and cut through the gold region, running from east to west, at irregular distances of fifteen to twenty, and perhaps some of them thirty miles apart.

Hence it appears that the gold veins are equally rich in all parts of that most remarkable section of country. Were it wanting, there are further proofs of this in the ravines and dry diggings, which uniformly confirm what nature so plainly shows in the rivers.

For the purpose of forming some opinion respecting the probable amount or value of treasure in the gold region, it will be proper to state the estimates which have been made of the quantity collected since its discovery

Gold was first discovered on the south fork of the American River, at a place called Sutter's Mill, now Culoma—late in May or early in June,

1848. Information which could be relied on announcing this discovery was not received in this city until late in the following autumn.

No immigration into the mines could, therefore, have taken place from the old States in that year. The number of miners was consequently, limited to the population of the Territory—some five hundred men from Oregon—Mexicans and other foreigners who happened to be in the country or came into it during the summer and autumn, and the Indians, who were employed by or sold their gold to the whites.

It is supposed there were not far from 5,000 men employed in collecting gold during that season. If we suppose they obtained an average of $1,000 each—which is regarded by well-informed persons as a low estimate—the aggregate amount will be $5,000,000.

Information of this discovery spread in all directions during the following winter; and, on the commencement of the dry season in 1849, people came into the territory from all quarters—from Chili, Peru, and other States on the Pacific coast of South America—from the west coast of Mexico—the Sandwich Islands, China and New Holland.

The emigration from the United States came in last, if we except those who crossed the Isthmus of Panama, and went up the coast in steamers, and a few who sailed early on the voyage round Cape Horn.

The American emigration did not come in by sea, in much force, until July and August, and that overland did not begin to arrive until the last of August and first of September. The Chilians and Mexican were early in the country. In the month of July it is supposed there were fifteen thousand foreigners in the mines. At a place called Sonorian Camp, it is believed there were at least ten thousand Mexicans. Hotels, restaurants, stores and shops of all descriptions, furnished whatever money could procure. Ice was brought from the Sierra, and ice-creams added to numerous other luxuries. An inclosure made of the trunks and branches of trees, and lined with cotton cloth, served as a sort of amphitheatre for bull-fights ; other amusements characteristic of the Mexicans were seen in all directions.

The foreigners resorted principally to the southern mines, which gave them a great superiority in numerical force over the Americans, and enabled them to take possession of some of the richest in that part of the country. In the early part of the season the Americans were mostly employed on the forks of the American and on Bear, Uba, and Feather rivers. As their numbers increased they spread themselves over the southern mines, and collisions were threatened between them and the foreigners. The latter, however, for some cause, either fear, or having satisfied their cupidity, or both, began to leave the mines late in August, and by the end of September many of them were out of the country.

It is not probable that during the first part of the season there were more than five or six thousand Americans in the mines. This would swell the whole number, including foreigners, to about twenty thousand the beginning of September. This period embraced about half of the season during which gold may be successfully collected in the rivers.

Very particular and extensive inquiries respecting the daily earnings and acquisitions of the miners lead to the opinion that they averaged an ounce per day. This is believed by many to be a low estimate ; but from the best information I was able to procure, I am of opinion that it approaches very near actual results. The half of the season, up to the 1st of September, would give sixty-five working days, and to each laborer, at $16 per ounce, $1,040. If, therefore, we assume $1,000 as the average collected by each laborer, we shall probably not go beyond the mark.

This would give an aggregate of $20,000,000 for the first half of the season—15,000,000 of which was probably collected by foreigners. During the last half of the season the number of foreigners was very much diminished, and, perhaps, did not exceed 5,000. At this time the American immigration had come in by land and sea, and the number of our fellow-citizens in the mines had, as was estimated, increased to between 40,000 and 50,000. They were most of them inexperienced in mining, and it is probable the results of their labors were not as great as has been estimated for the first part of the season and experienced miners, assuming that the average of half an ounce per day ought to be considered as reasonable, it would give an aggregate of about $20,000,000. If from this we deduct one-fourth on account of the early commencement of the wet season, we have an estimate of $15,000,000; at least five of which was collected by foreigners, who possessed many advantages from their experience in mining and knowledge of the country.

These estimates give, as the result of the operation in the mines for 1848 and 1849, the round sum of $40,000,000—one half of which was probably collected and carried out of the country by foreigners.

From the best information I could obtain, I am led to believe that at least $20,000,000 of the $40,000,000 were taken from the rivers, and that their richness has not been sensibly diminished, except in a few locations, which had early attracted large bodies of miners. This amount has principally been taken from the northern rivers, or those which empty into the Sacramento; the southern rivers, or those which flow into the San Joaquin, having been, comparatively, but little resorted to until near the close of the last season. These rivers are, however, believed, by those who have visited them, to be richer in the precious metal than those in the northern part of the gold region.

There is one river which, from *reported* recent discoveries, and not included in the description of those flowing into the great plain west of the Sierra Nevada, is as rich in gold as any of them. That is the *Trinity*, which rises north of the head waters of the Sacramento, and discharges into the Pacific not far from the fortieth degree of north latitude.

There are, as nearly as my recollection serves me, twelve principal rivers in which gold has been found ; but most of the $20,000,000 in the above estimate was taken from six or seven of them, where it was first discovered and most accessible.

Adopting the hypothesis that the gold found in the beds of these streams has been cut or worn from the veins in the quartz through which they have forced their way, and considering the fact that they are *all rich*, and are said to be nearly equally productive, we may form some idea of the vast amount of treasure remaining undisturbed in the veins which run through the masses of rock in various directions over a space of forty or fifty miles wide, and near five hundred miles long.

If we may be allowed to form a conjecture respecting the richness of these veins from the quantity of lump or coarse gold found in the dry diggings, where it appears to occupy nearly the same superfices it did originally in the rock—its specific gravity being sufficient to resist ordinary moving causes—we shall be led to an estimate almost beyond human calculation and belief. Yet, as far as I can perceive, there is no plausible reason why the veins which remain in the quartz may not be as valuable as those which have become separated from the decomposed rock. This matter can only be satisfactorily decided by actual discoveries.

The gold region of California having attracted a large share of public attention, it was to be expected that various suggestions and propositions would be made with respect to the proper mode of disposing of it.

The difficulty in arranging a suitable plan has been the want of accurate information on which a well considered opinion might be formed. Its distance from the seat of government, the conflicting statements and reports respecting it, served only to bewilder and mystify the public mind, and render a thorough examination of it necessary, to ascertain whether its value is such as to render legislation necessary for its proper protection and management.

If it appears, from the preceding part of this report, that it is sufficiently important to require laws suited to the condition and development of its wealth, we are necessarily brought to the consideration of the proper rules and regulations to be adopted for that purpose.

The survey and sale of that section of country, under our present land system, or any other mode which may be devised, would, undoubtedly, cause very serious discontent among those who have gone, and all who may desire to go there to collect gold, and a most unnecessary and unavoidable inequality in the distribution of wealth among the purchasers.

Sections and parts of sections of land, having no indications of gold on the surface, but possessing untold treasures in the bowels of the earth, might be sold for what would be a mere trifle in comparison of their real value. Capitalists would overbid the daring, strong-armed day-laborer, who had braved the storms of Cape Horn, or the privations of a journey across the plains ; and, by the power and combination of resources, would possess themselves of the most valuable mines which have been discovered, and employ skillful miners to examine the country with as much secrecy as possible, for the purpose of making such discoveries as would enable them in a great degree to monopolize the most valuable portions of the country.

It is much easier to imagine than describe the discontent, perhaps disorder, which would spring up among an hundred thousand freemen deprived the privilege of an equal enjoyment of, or participation in, what they have been in the habit of regarding as the common property of the people of the whole Union.

It is, perhaps, more than doubtful whether such laws could be enforced. The employment of troops for that purpose would not only be odious, but ineffectual; they would be more likely to set an example of insubordination, by desertion, than to compel obedience in others.

The people would unite with them in producing anarchy and confusion. No system, therefore, which is not in accordance with the interests of the people can be carried into successful operation. It is always fortunate when laws can be so framed as to harmonize those interests with the policy and duty of the government. It is believed that may be accomplished in this case.

While every American citizen in the mines is aware that he is on government property, and would consider any attempt to drive him away as an act of oppression, he at the same time feels that something is due from him for the privilege he enjoys, and he would willingly pay a reasonable sum to have those privileges defined, and to be protected in the enjoyment of them.

The gold in the rivers, the dry diggings and the ravines is accessible to any man who has the strength to use a pan or washer, a spade and pick-ax.

The employment of machinery may perhaps facilitate its collection, but it is not essential. Every man is master of his own movements. The case will be very different with the vein-mines, which yet remain in the rock. To work them successfully will require machinery, with horse or steam power, involving an expenditure of capital in proportion to the extent of the operations.

No prudent man will make such investments until his rights and privileges shall have been clearly defined by law. In the absence of all legal regulations, if a man were to discover a vein-mine and incur the

expense of erecting machinery to work it, any other person, citizen or
foreigner, might construct an establishment alongside of him, deprive
him of his discovery, and destroy the value of his property. Hence it
will be perceived that any law prescribing the privileges and duties of
miners should be so framed as to secure the rights of all.

There is some fertile soil in the gold region—beautiful valleys and
rich hill sides—which, under circumstances favorable to agriculture,
would undoubtedly be valuable for that purpose; but at present, and as
long as the collection of gold shall continue to reward labor so much
more abundantly than the cultivation of the soil, the important matter
to be considered is, the proper mode of disposing of the metallic wealth
of the country.

The first step, in my opinion, should be to reserve the entire region
where gold is found, from the operation of the pre-emption laws, and
from sale, so that it may be now regarded as the *common treasure* of the
American people, and hereafter as a rich inheritance to their posterity.
Then provide for the appointment of a commissioner of the mines, and a
sufficient number of assistant commissioners to carry the law into effect.

Let the office of the commissioner be established at some point convenient to the mines, say Sacramento Cicy, and the offices of his assistant on the principal rivers, and in the most productive districts. Provide that any and every American citizen, on application at the office of
the commissioner, or any of his assistants, and by paying one ounce, or
$16, or such sum as may be considered just and proper, shall be entitled
to receive a license or permit to dig anywhere in the Territory for one
year. Provide, also, that any one who shall *discover* or purchase of the
discoverer, a vein-mine, shall be entitled to work it, to a certain extent,
under proper regulations, on paying to the commissioner such per cent.
on the proceeds of the mine as may be a suitable tax on the privileges
granted. It will be necessary also to allow the miner to cut and use
such timber and other building materials as his business requires ; and,
also, to allow those who work under permits the privilege of erecting
cabins for shelter through the winter. Authorize the commissioner to
lay out sites for the towns in convenient situations to the mines, and offer
the lots for sale, reserving the metals and mineral, so that those who

make mining a permanent pursuit may accumulate around them the comforts and enjoyments of civilized life. Let those who desire to cultivate gardens or farm-lots be accommodated. It will be necessary also to authorize the sale of timber and other materials, for building and other purposes. There may be other suggestions which do not now occur to me, but no doubt will, to those who may be charged with the preparation of any measure which may be brought forward on this subject.

I have suggested one ounce or $16 as the price of a permit or license to dig or collect gold for one year. This I regard as about the average value of one day's labor in the mines. This tax on 50,000 miners, the probable number next summer, will give a revenue of $800,000. On 100,000 miners—the probable number of 1851—it will give $1,600,000, beside the per centum on the vein-mines, and the sum received for town lots, timbers, &c., &., which would probably swell the amount to at least $2,000,000. Any variation in the tax imposed will, of course, increase or diminish this estimate.

A suitable amount of the money thus collected should be expended in constructing roads and bridges, to facilitate communication to and through the mining districts.

These facilities will so reduce the cost of living in the mines, that the miners will instead of lose by paying the tax. These are accommodations which the miners themselves will ever provide, because of the want of concert of action among them sufficient to accomplish such objects, but for which they will willingly pay any moderate contribution. A liberal per centum should be allowed out of this sum, as a school fund, and for the establishment of an university to educate the youth of California. Let it not be considered that this will be doing injustice to the older States of the Union. They will reap a harvest sufficiently rich in their intercourse with their younger sister on the Pacific to justify the most liberal course of policy toward her.

I have given $20,000,000 as the probable revenue for 1851, under the proposed system. This would discharge the interest on the amount stipulated in the treaty to be paid to Mexico for California and New Mexico, provide $300,000 per annum for a school fund, and the necessary improvements in mining districts, and create a sinking fund of half a million per annum, to pay the principal of the indemnity to Mexico.

An increase of the number of miners, or of the price of permits, would of course increase the revenue. If the vein-mines shall be found as extensive and productive as the best-informed persons suppose, the right to work them, properly secured by law, and the opportunity thus offered of using machinery to advantage, will justify the collection of a much larger per cent. on their gross product than it is proposed to require from those who labor with their own hands in the use of the simple means now employed in the collection of gold. The amount, therefore, collected from this source may ultimately be as large, perhaps larger, than that for permits.

If revenue is an object, there can be little doubt that, by the adoption of this system, the amount collected in a few years will be larger than the entire district would command in ready money, if offered for sale; and the interests and privileges of those employed in the mines will be secured from the grasping and monopolizing spirit of individual proprietors; California and the whole Union preserved from scenes of anarchy and confusion, if not bloodshed, which must result from a sale of the mining region to speculators, and an attempt to protect them in the enjoyment of their purchases.

The salaries of the commissioner and his assistants may easily be paid out of the amount received, in fixed sums, or in the form of a per centum.

I have proposed to exclude foreigners from the privilege of purchasing permits, and from working as discoverers or purchasers in the vein-mines. My reasons for recommending this policy are, that these mines belong to, and in my judgment should be preserved for, the use and benefit of the American people. I mean, of course, all citizens, native and adopted.

During the mining season of 1849, more than 15,000 foreigners, mostly Mexicans and Chilenos, came in *armed bands* into the mining district, bidding defiance to all opposition, and finally carrying out of the country some $20,000,000 worth of gold dust, which belonged *by purchase* to the people of the United States. If not excluded by law, they will return and recommence the work of plunder. They may, with as much right, gather the harvest in the valley of the Connecticut, the Ohio, or Mississippi. No other nation, having the power to protect it, would permit its treasure to be thus carried away. I would not allow them to purchase permits, or work vein-mines, because the contributions proposed to be required are so moderate that they will not cause the slightest inconvenience to the miners, and are not designed as an equivalent for these privileges. Foreigners, therefore, would willingly pay these small sums for permission to collect and carry away millions of dollars in value. The object is not only a suitable revenue, but to preserve for the use of our own fellow-citizens the wealth of that region.

This system of permits will make all who purchase them *police officers, to aid in excluding* from the mines all who are not entitled to, or who do not procure them. This will prevent deserters from the army or navy from being harbored and protected in the mines. Not being allowed to purchase permits, the assistant commissioners, aided by the miners, would soon detect and arrest them. Sailors belonging to the mercantile marine would be detected in a similar manner, and thus prevented from running away.

The commerce of the country would be protected from the disastrous consequences resulting from the abandonment of ships by their crews, which necessarily imposes a heavy tax on consumers, because merchants, as a measure of self-protection, must charge such losses on their cargoes, and consequently they fall on those who purchase. The army and navy would be saved from demoralization, and prepared for service in case of necessity.

Many of the emigrants to California, especially those from the western States, will remain and form a resident population; but there will be thousands and tens of thousands of young and middle-aged workingmen from all parts of the Union, who will resort to the mines for the purpose of obtaining the means to purchase a farm or establish themselves in some favorite pursuit, and as soon as they have secured a sufficient amount will return, and their places will be supplied by others who will go and do likewise.

This process has already commenced. Many who went out last spring have returned with an ample reward for their labors and privations.

The market in California for the products and manufactures of the other States of the Union will enhance prices, which, with the gold collected and brought home by laboring people, will diffuse a degree of wealth and comfort hitherto unknown among them.

The *quicksilver mines* of California are believed to be numerous, extensive, and very valuable. There is one near San José, which belongs to, or is claimed by, Mr. Forbes of Tepic, in Mexico. The cinnabar ore, which produces the quicksilver, lies near the surface, is easily procured, and believed to be remarkably productive.

Discoveries of other mines are reported, but no certain information respecting them has been made public. It is, undoubtedly, a fortunate circumstance that nature, in bestowing on California such vast metallic treasure, has provided, almost in its immediate neighborhood, inexhaustible stores of quicksilver, which is so essential in gold mining.

The policy of government with respect to these mines of cinnabar should, in my opinion, be quite different from that which I have felt it my duty to suggest for the management of the gold region.

As soon as the necessary explorations can be made, and proper information obtained, it will be well to offer these mines for sale, and commit their development to the hands of private enterprise.

It is believed that there are extensive beds of silver, iron, and copper ores, in the Territory; but there is no information sufficiently accurate respecting them, to justify any statement of their existence or value.

I have already alluded to the propriety of establishing a mint in California. This is important in many respects. At this time there is not coin to supply a currency. Much difficulty is experienced in procuring enough to pay the duties on foreign goods. The common circulating medium is, therefore, gold dust, which is sold at $15 50 to $16 per ounce. In the mines it is frequently sold much lower. The miners, the laboring men, are the sufferers from this state of things.

Those who purchase and ship gold to the Atlantic States make large profits; *but those who dig lose what others make.*

I have estimated that there will be $5,000,000 collected during the current year. At $16 per ounce, that sum will weigh 3,125,000 ounces.

Gold at the United States Mint is worth $18 per ounce, making a difference in value on that quantity, between San Francisco and New York of $6,250,000, which would be saved to the miners by the establishment of a mint.

I have also suggested its importance as a means of promoting and increasing our trade with the west coast of Mexico and South America.

It is not doubted that the construction of a railway across the Isthmus of Panama, and perhaps the establishment of other lines of communication between the two oceans, will give to the products and manufactures of the older States of the Union command of the market of California to the exclusion, in a great degree, of those of the west coast.

A mint will therefore become of the utmost importance, to give such marketable value to silver bullion as to enable the merchants of those countries to keep up and increase their intercourse with our principal ports on the Pacific.

The silver bullion shipped to Europe from the west coast of Mexico amounts to more than ten millions of dollars per annum. From the countries on the west coast of South America, probably an equal quantity. That from Mexico goes to pay for European importations into her ports on the Atlantic side.

A market at San Francisco for this bullion will be the means of substituting American and Chinese fabrics for those of European manufacture in all those countries. This will greatly increase the trade between China and California.

I have the honor to be, with great respect, your most obedient servant,   [Signed]

T. BUTLER KING.

To Hon. JOHN M. CLAYTON, Secretary of State.

Library of Congress Cataloguing in Publication Data

Taylor, Bayard, 1825-1878.
Eldorado, or, Adventures in the path of empire.
(Classics of the Old West)
Reprint. Originally published: New York: G. P. Putnam: London R. Bentley, 1850.
1. California—Gold discoveries.
2. California—Description and travel—1848-1869.
3. Voyages to the Pacific coast.
4. Mexico—Description and travel. 5. Taylor, Bayard, 1825-1878.
I. Title. II. Title: Eldorado
F865.T23   1983   979.4'04   83-4285
ISBN 0-8094-4626-X (library) (v. 2)
ISBN 0-8094-4625-1 (retail) (v. 2)

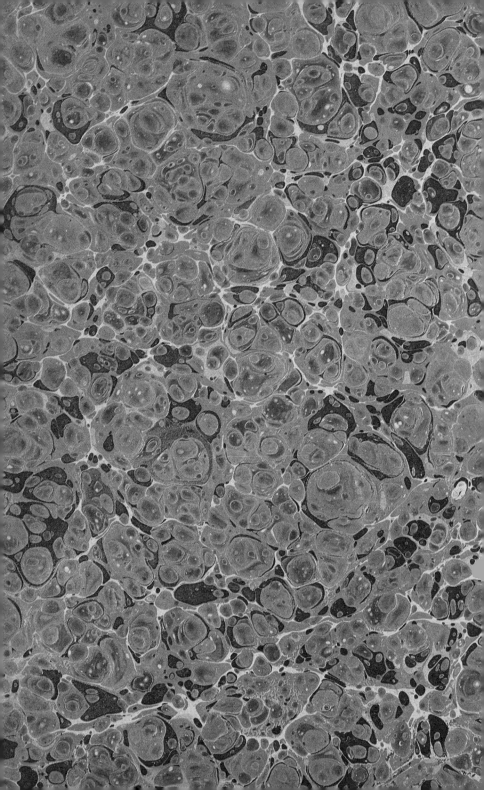